A NORTH LAWNDALE JOURNEY OF FAITH:

THE TESTIMONY OF AN EX-OFFENDER

To Carl
God Bless

Love

Stanley

A NORTH LAWNDALE JOURNEY OF FAITH:

THE TESTIMONY OF AN EX-OFFENDER

BY STANLEY T. RATLIFF

"Now faith is the substance of things hoped for,
the evidence of things not seen."
—Hebrews 11:1 KJV

CELESTIAL MINISTRIES PRESS
CHICAGO

Praise for A North Lawndale Journey of Faith:
The Testimony of an Ex-Offender

*In A North Lawndale Journey of Faith: The Testimony of an Ex-Offender,
Stanley Ratliff takes us into the real and unvarnished territory of his life
to share a glimpse of what it means to live in and love a neighborhood
that many people write off. Despite being victimized by systemic injustice
and racism, Stanley's story reveals courage, faith, a loving family, friends,
mentors, and a heartfelt hope to find good in all people. This book provides
a clear picture of what a true life of faith can overcome and shows that
overwhelming obstacles are often stepping stones in transforming ourselves
and the community around us.*

-**Anne Rand**, Program Facilitator | Long-term Solutions Advocate
Willow Creek Care Center

*I first met my dear friend Stanley Ratliff thirty years ago. I have always had the
greatest admiration for him. He has a deep love for God, his wife Antoinette,
and his three sons. He has a desire to lead people into a relationship with
Jesus Christ through his powerful music ministry. Stanley's example and life
story will greatly bless and encourage you. I highly recommend this book.*

-**Carey Casey**, Shepherding Pastor, Lawndale Community Church,
Chicago, IL and CEO, Championship Fathering

*Stanley Ratliff's story shows us how the life of a young man growing up in
North Lawndale can unfold with hope and purpose rather than despair
and destruction, bearing fruit from his labors instead of heartache and
pain. His testimony illustrates how his faith grew stronger with each trial,
hardship, and difficulty, bringing courage to the reader. We gain insight
into how powerfully God intervenes in the life of one who chooses to follow
His leading. No journey in life is easy, but very few men choose to live one
of sacrifice as Stanley has in his desire to see children and his neighborhood
changed for the good. This story is a treasure for all who have asked if their
life can make a difference. It changes us, changes neighborhoods, and has the
potential to inspire positive outcomes in the face of sometimes overwhelming
challenges.*

-**Mary Johnson** Prison Fellowship Field Director for Illinois &
Wisconsin

Published by Celestial Ministries Press
2149 S. Drake Ave.
Chicago, IL 60623

Manufactured in the United States of America
Interior Design by: Arlana Johnson
Cover Design by: Designs by Triv

ISBN: 978-0-578-87386-2

Dedication

This book is dedicated to the memories of the late Mr. Bill Barnhart and Mr. Ozzie Porter, Sr. Both men went to be with the Lord in 2020. Each loved and cherished their families and graciously extended that same love to me and mine. They were father figures not just for Anoinette and I, but for all three of our sons as well. They shall forever remain in out hearts.

"O God, you have taught me from my earliest childhood, and I constantly tell others about the wonderful things you do. Now that I am old and gray, do not abandon me, O God. Let me proclaim your power to this new generation, your mighty miracles to all who come after me."

—*Psalm 71:17-18 NLT*

Contents

Acknowledgments

First, I want to thank my Lord and Savior Jesus Christ, God the Father, and the Holy Spirit for helping me to write this book, which was planted deep within me. I'd also like to thank my editor, Mark Boone, who saw merit in my manuscript and agreed to shepherd me through each step of the process of getting it published. Thanks also to Teshauna Edwards and Danzella Graham, who helped me to compile and collate the pictures for this book. A special thanks to my family—my wife Antoinette; sons, Andrew, Antwane, and Antonio, and my sisters and brothers. A big thanks to my mother Linnie Ratliff, who helped to clarify events from my early life and also provided many pictures that I never knew she had. Thanks also, to the very special friends whom God has placed in my life and who have supported me and Celestial Ministries throughout the years: Pat Ford and the Stein Family Foundation, my St. Malachy School family, Denise and John Burns, Mary Cray and Phil Janicak, Bill and Nan Barnhart, The Roscoe Company, Mary Johnson and Prison Fellowship, Anne Rand and the Willow Creek Church, Christ Church of Oak Brook, Tom and Faith Kennington, Paul Newman and the Timothy Project, Paul Isihara and family, the board members of Celestial Ministries, Mike Trout and YMEN, Deacon Benjamin and Lois Benjamin, Dave and Lisa Wilcoxon, Dr. Wayne "Coach" Gordon and the Lawndale Christian Community Church, the men from my Bible study Group (Men's Fraternity), and all of my friends in the North Lawndale community.

Foreword

I first met Stanley Ratliff in 1975 and had the privilege of coaching him in football at Farragut High School. I noticed him immediately and saw him as an attentive, hard-working, dedicated young man whose desire to improve and get ahead set him apart from the pack. Stanley was easy to coach because he always strived to do his best. Thus began our nearly five-decades-long friendship.

As a single person living in North Lawndale, I didn't know too many people when I came directly out of Wheaton College. It was these football players who became my friends. We started the Fellowship of Christian Athletes Bible study of which Stanley was a leader from the very beginning. I spent most of my free time with these Christian athletes—from eating dinner at McDonald's at night, attending weekend outings to watch college football games, and going on camping trips.

In 1976, we bought a weight machine and fixed up an old storefront behind which I lived. The Farragut athletes—especially the football players—would come and lift weights to grow stronger. It was during these times in the weight room that Stanley's leadership continued to grow and shine as he brought new people to the weight room and to attend our FCA Bible study. Stanley has always been willing to tell people about the Lord Jesus Christ.

After he graduated from high school, our paths diverged but we remained in touch. When he became ensnared in the criminal justice system—a classic case of being in the wrong place at the wrong time—he immediately reached out to me. I went with him often to court and visited him several times when he was away in prison. We had weekly phone calls during which he would read a poem or sing a song that he had written, share Bible verses, as well as pray together. Though we were apart, our relationship grew deeper.

One of my fondest moments was when Stanley was granted clemency by former Governor of Illinois Jim Edgar, largely because of his fiancée Antoinette's tireless efforts on his behalf. She and a few of Stanley's supporters that included me testified before the clemency board about the circumstances that led to Stanley's conviction and how he was wrongfully incarcerated. As a result, he was granted clemency and released. I had the privilege, along with my four-year-old son Austin, to drive to Dixon, Illinois, to pick him up and return him to his family. It was a great day, and one of the happiest moments was watching his son Antonio run into his arms when he returned home. The following Sunday, Stanley and Antoinette were wed during our Sunday morning worship service.

Stanley has been a positive influence at Lawndale Christian Community Church and the entire North Lawndale community since that day. His story, recorded in the pages of this memoir, has been told countless times and has blessed thousands of people immensely.

Watching Stanley live his life these past decades has been like seeing one miracle performed after another. His life story is as true as it is inspiring. My life has been blessed immeasurably by knowing Stanley. By reading this book, yours will be also. It is a genuine story about the ups and downs that we all face, yet with God's help, we are able to overcome and even flourish.

I am extremely thankful for Stanley's life and his love for family, community, and our Lord Jesus Christ, and I am so thankful to call him my friend.

Dr. Wayne "Coach" Gordon, Founding Pastor
Lawndale Christian Community Church
Loving God. Loving People.
2021

Growing Up in North Lawndale

"For we walk by faith, not by sight." —*2 Corinthians 5:7 NKJV*

I've been a person of faith since I was a child. When I was about eight years old, whenever I would leave the house, I'd walk the streets with my head down, searching the ground for a coin here or there, and about eighty percent of the time I would find one. Sometimes it was only a penny, but nevertheless, it was still money. This became a habit, and I figured out that, by looking for coins when there was no guarantee that I'd find one, I was exercising my growing faith. Even at that young age, I knew that God was with me.

Before that, at the age of five, my siblings and I would watch "The Ten Commandments," "The Robe," and "Ben Hur" when they were aired on TV around Easter time. Watching these epic movies gave me my first insight that there was a God. The miracles that were displayed in these movies inspired me at a young age to live my life as if this awesome God really did exist, prophesied by the scripture: *"Come near to God and he will come near to you"* *(James 4:8) NIV.*

My Father, Arthur Earl Ratliff

I can remember several things about my father, Arthur Earl Ratliff. He and my mom were both from Grenada, Mississippi. He was a veteran of World War II, and after the war in 1948, as part of the Great Migration, they got married and moved to Chicago the following year. From their union nine children were born: Margaret, Mildred, Gloria, Arthur, Lynette, Janice, Aljose, myself, and Randy. My mother told me there would have actually been eleven of us had she not miscarried one child and lost another during the first month of his birth.

My father and my uncle Walter, (my mother's brother), began working at Pettibone Manufacturing, a company that made heavy metal machines, located at Cicero Avenue and Division Street where the Coca-Cola Company is now. He worked there for 30 years before retiring.

I used to think that he worked at a bakery because he would always bring home pastries. I only recently learned from my mother that he volunteered during his lunch break in the cafeteria, where he got the pastries that he would bring us. He was a good man except when he got drunk, and it seemed like every Friday after he got paid, he would get drunk. His favorite drink was "Old Grand-Dad."

I would walk home after school, and by the time I would get to the corner where I lived, I would see several police cars, and I knew immediately that they were at my house. After all, my dad and my mother would frequently get into arguments or fights.

One day, my mother was so fed up that she threw some hot water on my dad and scalded him. Another time when I got home, I found out that my father and my oldest sister Margaret had gotten into a fight. Once again, the police were called. I think the whole police department in the 10th district where I lived knew our last name fairly well because each policeman probably came to our house at one time or another.

I also remember that my father loved baseball and was a loyal fan of the Chicago Cubs. Sometimes he would make us watch the Cubs play, and we weren't allowed to say a word as long as the game was on. Although I'm not much of a baseball fan, I can remember Ernie Banks, Ron Santo, Glenn Becker, Randy Hundley, Don Kessinger, and Billy Williams—star players in the late 1960s and early 1970s.

As a child, the only place I can remember my father ever taking us was to Midway Airport to watch the planes take off and land. Midway Airport was only 25 minutes away from our home. I don't remember him taking us to Disney World, Great America, Riverview, or even to nearby Douglass Park.

Despite these shortcomings, he was a good father because he took care of our family. We always had a roof over our heads, food on the table, and clean clothes to wear. He was also the disciplinarian of the family and would whip all of us with a brown coral-encrusted leather belt. My mother often had to step in and say, "That's enough!" because it seemed as if he didn't know when to stop.

I remember walking down the street one day with a nail in my hand defacing cars as I walked. By the time I made it to the alley, a man stopped me and asked, "Son, what's your name?" When I told him, he asked me where I lived, and I gave him my address. After a week had passed, and I thought I was out of hot water, on a Sunday evening there was a knock on my door. It was the man who had stopped me from vandalizing cars that day. He told my mother that one of her sons had been defacing cars on the block with a nail. He had lost the paper on which he had written the name of the culprit. My mother called each of us by name one by one. At the time, I was in the bathtub taking a bath.

She called Joe, and he came. "No, that's not him," the man said. Then she called Randy. "That's not him either," he said. Finally, she said, "Stanley Ted, bring your ass out here right now!" I got out of the tub half wet with the towel around my waist. "Yep, that's him!" the man said.

My father gave me a whipping that I will never forget, using the brown leather belt on me for the last time. Before that last whipping, I would put on a double layer of clothes to insulate myself from the blows, but for this last one, clad only in my underwear, I didn't have a chance. *"When I was a child, I talked like a child, I thought like a child, I reasoned like a child. When I became a man, I put the ways of childhood behind me" (1 Corinthians 13:11) NIV.*

My Mother, Linnie Marie Ratliff

My mother, Linnie Marie Ratliff, is a sweet woman, so I really couldn't see how she ended up with my father. Yet, we can't always see what another person sees in someone else. I'm sure my father had some love in him. It's just that I didn't see it, or at least could not feel it at the time. She comes from a pretty big family with 14 sisters and brothers, all of whom migrated to such major cities as Chicago, Milwaukee, Detroit, and Sacramento.

My mother had to overcome much adversity and ended up raising all nine of us by herself. She worked in shipping and receiving as a merchandise marker at Sears Roebuck and Company at Homan and Arthington Streets on the West Side for 28 years until it was closed down and she was transferred to the location at North and Harlem Avenue until she retired in 1991.

My mom was always there when we needed help with anything. I used to enjoy waking up early in the morning to the aroma of flapjacks and bacon, sometimes mackerel. The smell of food was always in the air. While I had never seen her wash clothes, we always had clean clothes to wear to school. I guess she must have done it while we were sleeping.

As we grew up and began to experience life, she was always there to support us and never held us back. She always taught us to be respectful to adults and to do what's right, heeding the wisdom of Proverbs 22:6: *"Train up a child in the way he should go: and when he is old, he will not depart from it"* NKJV.

She'd tell us, "When someone offers you something, it's OK to say no sometimes." Or, " Always say, 'thank you' when someone gives you something."

She'd admonish us not to stay too long when visiting a friend's house so that we don't overstay our welcome, to always raise the seat when using the toilet, to be sure to flush it when finished, to never take anything that didn't belong to us, and to never bring more than one girlfriend to the house.

The last admonition I heard from her was when my sister Janice had two boyfriends. She had broken up with one and ended up going with another one. Both of these guys were on the football team at different high schools.

One day, they both showed up at our home and started fighting, breaking the downstairs door to our apartment, but no one was hurt. After this fight, I understood what my mother meant by not having more than one girlfriend over to the house. These simple nuggets helped me along in life.

At one point during my adolescence, it was just my mother and me living in the apartment while I was attending college. She never made me get a job even though I had turned 18. I always worked during the summer so that I could help her with the bills.

Joining the William Penn Elementary School Band

In third grade I joined the band at William Penn Elementary School under the direction of Mr. George Paris. He'd taught many students how to play different instruments, and Penn had the best band on the West Side of Chicago.

Being in this band taught us discipline and punctuality. We all got along very well and were proud to be in the band. I remember playing such musical selections as "Peter and the Wolf," "Under the Double Eagle," and "The Star-Spangled Banner." These songs will forever be in my heart, as will my Penn School bandmates. Four of my cousins were in the band: Walter McClain, Jo Ann McClain, Benny McClain, and Thomas McClain, as well as Janet

King and Douglas Scott, who played clarinet; Stan Shingles who played trumpet; Princella Walker, who played trombone; Glenn Gatewood, who played the French horn, while I played the tenor saxophone.

At Penn I was also a patrol boy and felt immensely proud to be one. My job was to assist the crossing guard helping students cross the streets. As a patrol boy, it made me feel incredibly special because I also got to attend class a little later than the other students.

On the way to school, my cousins Billy and Michael Avery and I would sing songs that we would make up, one of which was called "We're Jaywalking," and we improvised it as we were crossing in the middle of the street. Afterwards, I would head to my assigned patrol post without even giving a second thought to the fact that I had just violated a law.

In 1971, when I was in the sixth grade, my father died of a heart attack on the corner at 12th and Harding, where he hung out. I remember clearly having a conversation with God, not knowing what the outcome would be. I told God that I wanted *Him* to be my Father, and sure enough, He has been that to me, holding true to the scripture: *"As a father has compassion on his children, so the LORD has compassion on those who fear him"* *(Psalm 103:13) NIV.*

At the time, He protected me from all harm, and I didn't have one fight in school. None of the gangs bothered me or tried to recruit me. God had provided my family and I with a place to live, kept food on our table, and saved us from three different house fires growing up.

He had also helped me to earn good grades in school and find favor with teachers. I was blessed because three teachers at Penn: Mrs. Mary Cray, Mr. Charles Weir, and Mr. David Grogan would spend extra time with a group of students and me. Almost every weekend they would take us outside of the neighborhood to their homes, on camping trips, to see the Milwaukee Bucks play, and other places. I knew we were considered special because none of the other children had ever been outside of North Lawndale. Our parents didn't take us anywhere because they were either always working or they just didn't have the money. We were poor, but we didn't live like we were poor.

We had fun as kids and were resourceful, using our God-given creativity to make our own toys: slingshots, go karts, top shooters, and the list goes on. For sports we played basketball, football, softball, or "strike 'em out," a game that no one plays anymore—a game where you would pitch a rubber ball as fast as you can into a square box, and the batter would challenge you by trying to hit the ball. Other games we played were "Tag" (It), "Johnny Come Across," and "Hide and Seek." These games were fun and brought unity to our community. The girls played "hopscotch," jumped rope, both single and Double Dutch, and played hand games such as "A Sailor Went to Sea, Sea, Sea," and others. There were gangs, but they weren't shooting and killing each other like they do today. Back then, gangs fought with their fists and sometimes with bats, but hardly ever with guns.

Winning Second Place in an Essay Contest

When I reached the eighth grade, a few students from my class entered an essay contest on black history hosted by the DuSable Museum. It was by faith and the Holy Spirit (although I didn't know it at the time) that guided me in writing the essay. I can't quite remember the title of my essay, but I do remember that I came in second place. In doing so, I was invited to a reception dinner at the DuSable Museum and was given two tickets to attend. I can clearly remember my oldest sister Mildred taking me. At the ceremony, they called my name, and I received a certificate signed by the museum's founder, the late Margaret Burroughs, and a carved statue from Africa. I felt good and special, knowing that my Father had allowed this to happen. Once again, it was a manifestation of faith for me, as the Bible clearly says:

"And without faith it is impossible to please God, because anyone who comes to him must believe that he exists and that he rewards those who earnestly seek him" (Hebrews 11:6) NIV.

Attending Farragut High School

"You will seek me and find me when you seek me with all your heart." —Jeremiah 29:13 NIV

After graduating from eighth grade, I began playing basketball over the summer. I wanted to learn how to play because all of my friends played. I hadn't learned the game because I was too busy playing other sports like football, baseball, and strike 'em out. I also played the tenor saxophone, but over the summer, it was all basketball all the time. Every day in the morning, noon, and evenings, I was playing basketball somewhere.

I was now beginning to rely on my faith more often, and when it was time to try out for the freshman basketball team at my high school, David Glasgow Farragut, located at 2345 S. Christiana, I asked my Heavenly Father to help me make the team. At that time Farragut was the only high school that served the North Lawndale community.

I had the tryout and made the team, but all of my friends who had played basketball from third grade through eighth grade didn't. They kept asking how on earth I was able to make the team when they didn't. I replied without a shadow of doubt, that it was God. I knew it had to be because of Him because I was scared, even though I was determined. I trusted Him, and He made it happen as recorded in Proverbs 3:5,6 NIV: *"Trust in the LORD with all of your heart and lean not on your own understanding; in all your ways submit to him, and he will make your paths straight."*

Many of us miss out on the blessings and opportunities that God has in store for us because we don't know who He is and what He is capable of. We may know that He created us, yet we never turn to Him and ask Him for assistance. God loves us, He cares for us, and He wants to give us the desires of our hearts. He gives each of us a measure of faith, but the question is whether we're using it.

I believe that faith is like a muscle and needs to be exercised. If we never use it, it will never grow, but the more we use it, the stronger it gets. Being on the basketball team helped me to adjust to high school, but what helped me the most was being in the male chorus at Farragut.

The Farragut High School Male Chorus

When I went to try out for the band in high school, to my surprise, there wasn't a band like I had known at William Penn. It was composed of about six students, and they sounded terrible! They didn't even have an instrument for me to play. The band teacher invited me to join them, but I told him, "No, thank you." Forty years later, I found out that other students from my grammar school band felt the same way as I did at the time.

A bandmate of mine, Janet King, said she experienced the same thing when she tried out for the Farragut High School Band. We laughed because we had an awesome band at Penn, but in high school, it was a different story. I loved music, so I ended up joining the male chorus, one of the best decisions I made in high school.

First of all, I already knew a few guys who were in the chorus—my cousins Billy and Michael Avery, as well as Tyrone Powell, Calvin Ford, John Campbell, and a host of football players. We had a great director in Mr. John Ghans. We had fun, but when it came time for competing and performing, we got serious. We never earned a rating below superior when it came to competitions, and our spring concerts were sold out because everyone wanted to hear the male chorus.

Once, we had a concert and football practice at the same time, and our football coach Mr. Steele, told us that we needed to be at practice, while Mr. Ghans insisted that we be at the performance. He didn't seem to care what Coach Steele had said, we'd better be at the performance prepared to sing. I don't remember any one of us attending football practice. Everyone was at the performance. Coach Steele even came to hear us and apologized to Mr. Ghans.

I really enjoyed the songs that we sang in the male chorus because most of them were either Negro Spirituals or well-known hymns. God was still in the mix, even though I wasn't attending church regularly at the time. I hadn't been attending because my mother had stopped forcing us to go. When my brothers, cousins, and I were younger, she made us go every Sunday. When we would walk to church, a friend of ours, "Baby Bass," would embarrass us by shouting out our last names in a joking way: "Ratliff, Avery, Fullove, Sykes"! When he did it, everyone knew we were headed to church. Little did we know that God was using our family as a light to shine and to let people in the community see that they should have been going to church, too. Although we didn't always understand what the preacher was saying all the time, God's Word never goes void, as proclaimed in Isaiah 55:11, *"So is my word that goes out from my mouth: it will not return to me empty, but will accomplish what I desire and achieve the purpose for which I sent it" NIV.*

Trying Out for Football

When basketball season was over and as I was walking into the school's lunchroom, I saw several guys wearing nice football jerseys, and I wanted one mainly because they looked good and

11

everyone would stare at the athlete who was wearing one of them. Moreover, the girls flocked around the guys when they wore their jerseys, so I asked my Heavenly Father to help me get on the football team. Here I go again, exercising my faith. I had played flag football in the streets, but I had never played contact football that required wearing pads and helmets. I really wanted one of those jerseys and was willing to do whatever it took to get one.

The first part was easy. All we did was conditioning. We had to run around the gym about twenty times and did a lot of sprints. Each day you could see the guys who were trying out falling off one by one because they weren't used to conditioning. I was used to it because of my playing on the basketball team. I refused to give up because I wanted to wear one of those jerseys. Finally, after a week of conditioning, I made the team. Now, I had to be taught to learn how to play the game.

The head coach, Coach Guido Marchetti, put me in two positions: offensive and defensive end. On offense, I had to learn how to run patterns and catch the ball. On defense, I had to learn how to string the play out and make sure that no opponent got on the outside of me.

At first it was a struggle playing defensive end because somehow everyone would always beat me. All I could hear when this happened was, "RATLIFF!"

I knew I had made a mistake, but I had to learn how to play that position.

In my first game, I got hit so hard that I didn't know what had hit me. I could hardly catch my breath, and I heard somebody say that I had gotten the wind knocked out of me. After lying on the field for nearly five minutes, someone helped me to the sideline, and after a few plays, I went back in.

My Mentor and Coach, Wayne Gordon

During my second year, our assistant coach, Wayne Gordon, was a young man who had just graduated from Wheaton College. We were able to relate to him more than we could to all our other coaches because he was only about four or five years older than most of us. He was also a classroom teacher, unlike the other coaches. We started calling him "Coach" because he was our football coach and we considered him a friend. We felt like he was on our level and that he understood us more. He even told us that he wanted to move into our neighborhood, to which we replied, "Coach you don't want to live here! There aren't any whites living in our neighborhood!" But he didn't listen to us. Instead, he'd listened to God and ended up moving into the neighborhood anyway.

Coach Gordon didn't move in the part of the neighborhood where we lived. Instead, he moved closer to where Farragut was located in the 3100 block west on 15th Place, which was around the corner from the "Bucket of Blood."

According to North Lawndale legend, several murders occurred in this corner tavern. The legend that gave the place its name involved a man who came in, sat down at the bar, and ordered a drink for himself and for "her," too, as he pointed to the head of a woman that he had just decapitated and set on the bar. By the time Coach Gordon had moved to the neighborhood, it was no longer called the "Bucket of Blood." It had become a neighborhood store.

One day Coach Gordon, I, and another person had gone to this store. As we were in line waiting to pay for our items, a man came in with a knife arguing with the man standing in front of us. I grabbed Coach and my friend, and we exited without any one of us getting hurt. Once again, it was God giving me wisdom on what to do. As James says chapter 1 verse 5 NIV, *"If any of you lacks wisdom, you should ask God, who gives generously to all without finding fault, and it will be given to you."*

God had given me wisdom that day to get out of harm's way, and because of Him, I also made the honor roll throughout high school and became the president of the National Honor Society at Farragut.

A Losing Season

In 1975, we lost every football game but one. I remember the coaches taking us to play a game at Ridgeland High School, a school located in the far northwestern suburbs. It was raining when we got there, and the freshman team had just finished playing. They lost their game 32-0. We told them not to worry, that we would get them. As we entered the field, all 23 of us ran out and began stretching. All of a sudden, we heard the band playing as if it was a college game.

While the band played, the people in the stands began to cheer. The next thing we saw were these huge football players circling the field. It seemed as if they would never stop coming. It had to have been 50 or 60 of them. They were better built than we were and there were more of them than us. When the game started, they began smashing us as if we were little kids. They were executing plays that we had never seen before, and we lost 56-0—and in the rain! I will never forget the drubbing as long as I live.

After the game, I went downtown to see the movie "Cinderella," also known as "The Other Cinderella," an adult movie that I shouldn't have been allowed to see but was admitted to anyway. I was wearing a long army coat and hat and I sat in the front row, incognito or so I thought. I watched the movie scooting down in my seat so that no one would see me. About halfway through the movie, I heard someone whisper, "Ratliff, Ratliff!" I turned around to see five guys from the football team. We laughed and laughed. I guess after being beaten so badly, we all felt like going to see a movie to divert ourselves from the brutal loss.

Years later I realized that if I were going to follow Christ, I couldn't have one foot in and one foot out. I had to go all in and would have to surrender all to Him. Of course, at this time in my life I was still in the world, but I thank God now that I've made up my mind to follow Him and let Him lead my life. *"Him who hath called you out of darkness into his marvellous light" (1 Peter 2:9) KJV.*

A Deepening Relationship with Coach Gordon

A few of us used to visit Coach Gordon at his apartment after football practice to make sure he was all right. That's when he decided that we should have Bible study, which he decided to call the FCA (Fellowship of Christian Athletes). It was my very first time studying the Bible and understanding what it meant to follow Jesus.

Although I had gone to church when I was younger, I never opened a Bible or attended Bible study. It was then that I accepted Jesus Christ as my personal Lord and Savior as recorded in Romans:10:9: *"That if you declare with thy mouth, "Jesus is Lord," and believe in your heart that God raised Him from the dead, you will be saved" NIV.*

I was now a child of God adopted into His family and became a new creation. The new things have come; the old things have gone; the new is here, according to 2 Corinthians 5:17 NIV.

Coach used to take our group to football games at Wheaton College, and he would have a huge bag of "birdseed" for us to munch on. (We didn't know anything about trail mix then.) He also persuaded us to participate in a FCA summer football camp, which was fun. We listened to former NFL players share their testimonies about being Christian athletes, and from there, I wanted to become one as well.

Football players from rival Marshall High School also attended the camp, so we got to know each other personally. When we played against each other during conference games, we were able to call each other by name. This was different because at all of the other games we played, we didn't know our opponents' names.

Coach also recruited us to sing Christmas carols at a mental health center down the street from his apartment. I guess you can call this community service, but we were only doing it because he had asked us to. Community service wasn't mandatory when we were in high school like it is now. I'm glad we did it because it fulfilled the call of Philippians 2:3-4, NIV, which states: *"Do nothing out of selfish ambition or vain conceit. Rather, in humility value others above yourselves, not looking to your own interests but each of you to the interests of the others."*

It felt good singing Christmas carols to the people at the center because we could tell that they appreciated it. Some of them didn't have families to visit them during the Christmas season, so when they experienced a group of young athletes singing for them, they were as delighted as we were to sing.

Coach Gordon also took us to visit suburban churches as well as churches in the neighborhood. For the first time in my life, my eyes were opened to how differently people worshiped. Some churches worshiped very quietly so that you could hear a pin drop. Others praised God with music that was very settled, while others worshiped Him with loud music during services that seemed as though they would never end, much as according to the Apostle Paul: *"But what does it matter? The important thing is that in every way, whether from false motives or true, Christ is preached. And because of this I rejoice"* (Philippians 1:18) NIV.

We all appreciated Coach Gordon for taking the time to introduce us to these different churches.

Our Undefeated Season

In my senior year, our football team went undefeated with a record of 9-0. We had a blast the whole season. The male chorus attended all of the games to cheer us on. We made it to the semi-finals but lost to Chicago Vocational High School, a football powerhouse. Because we had been beating our opponents by 30 or 40 points, we didn't know how to take the loss. Some of the same plays that northwest suburban Ridgeland had executed to defeat us, we had started using against our opponents, CVS included. In that final game though, our team fumbled the ball on the four-yard line. Our captain Andrew Moore went to the sideline and told the coach to take out our quarterback because he was intoxicated. After that, everything went downhill, ending in the loss that also ended my high-school football career.

Organizing Our Farragut High School Reunion

Every year on the last Saturday in July, Farragut holds a reunion in Douglass Park. The reunion is for all of Farragut's classes, but community residents and alumni from other west side high schools also participate in it. What makes the reunion so special is that it is always peaceful. The community comes together with the old schoolers and the new schoolers all in one place, having a great time. We enjoy each other's company, and it's always a pleasure seeing someone who we haven't seen in a long time.

At one of the reunions a couple of people who had graduated in my class of 1977 asked why we hadn't had a reunion of our own class in a while. It had been 34 years since the last one, and our class hadn't had one since. I told them that if they wanted to have one that I would help them. I knew quite a few alumni from our class and how to get in touch with some of them.

By faith and trusting in God, I convened a meeting with a small group of them, and we had our thirty-sixth reunion at the Marriott Hotel Midway. My former vocal group "Superior Movement," which my friends and I formed while attending Farragut and which I describe in more detail in the next chapter, was the entertainment for the event. We were joined by my classmate and friend Joe Soto, a well-known radio personality from the local V103 radio station. Joe always supported me whenever I needed him for an event.

I had to convince the band that we could do it, and we did. By that time, Tyrone lived in California, and Wayne lived in

Alabama. Everyone else lived in Chicago or one of its suburbs. We performed as though we had never missed a beat.

My cousin Billy was the mastermind at contacting everyone and calling the rehearsals. It was just like old times, the arguing, the coming to rehearsal late, but still having the same goal of putting on a great show. My cousin Michael Avery also sang a song with us as well.

Because the reunion had been a success, the group of alumni that had planned the last reunion, decided to have a fortieth reunion. Superior Movement agreed to sing again, except that the group wanted to perform at a joint reunion for the Class of 1977 and the group's reunion itself. The group had lots of followers, and the committee wanted them to see us perform once again. We had reached an agreement, and the class of 1977 would be celebrating its fortieth year reunion and at the same time, Superior Movement would be celebrating its fortieth year as a vocal group.

From Male Chorus to Local Celebrity

"I know the plans I have for you," announces the LORD. "I want you to enjoy success. I do not plan to harm you. I will give you hope for the years to come." —Jeremiah 29:11 NIRV

While attending Farragut, my friends and I started "Superior Movement," a vocal quintet. We had idolized a vocal group called "The Black Emeralds" and used to watch them sing at the school, so we got together and started our own singing group. We were all members of the male chorus and attended William Penn Elementary School.

The group members who competed in our first talent contest were: Michael Avery, Calvin Ford, Tyrone Powell, William Unger and me. After much practice, we were ready and chose to sing a song that had been recorded by the Stylistics titled "Miracles." William sang the first lead, and Michael sang the second lead. We sounded like the recording and had the girls in the audience screaming. Suddenly, we became local celebrities, attracting girls to our rehearsals.

At the second talent show, we flopped. When the band started playing, we ended up singing in the wrong place. This made both Michael and William upset, and both ended up leaving the group.

We searched for their replacements, and Michael's brother Billy and a freshman, David Williams, joined the group. With the new line-up, we were able to book gigs all over Chicago. Every talent show that we had entered had us in first place. Soon, we began opening acts for such big names as The Chi-lites The Dells, the late James Brown, the late Phyllis Hyman, Eddie Murphy, Stephanie Mills, and Ray, Goodman, and Brown, among others.

In 1981, we recorded our very first single, "For You," a remake by the late well-known composer and arranger Van McCoy. When we first heard it on the radio, we couldn't believe it. Everyone around the neighborhood congratulated us, telling us that they heard our song.

Our second single, "Wide Shot," was released in 1982. The song went to Number 18 on the Billboard Charts, and was played on radio stations all over the United States, but we didn't like the song because the producers wouldn't allow us to record our own material before its release. After the song was released, we decided to call a meeting with the producers before we went back into the studio. We wanted to sing some of the songs we had written for the next album, but they refused to honor our request, and we had a falling out that resulted in our being black-balled in the industry.

The experience took a toll on us because in our youthful naivete, we were not mindful of the scripture from 1 Peter 5:8, NIV, which tells us: *"Be alert and of sober mind. Your enemy the devil prowls around like a roaring lion looking for someone to devour."*

Taken in by a Hoax

At the time a young lady claiming to be the niece of the president of the popular local radio station, WMBX, alleged that her uncle was close friends with the then CEO of Motown Records. She had made a deal with Tyrone of our group that if he agreed to marry her, she would send the CEO a demo tape that we had recorded in an attempt to get an audition. Our manager then sent bios of the group to the executive at Motown but never got a reply. Tyrone kept calling the woman and her uncle, explaining to them that no one was contacting us. Finally, one day a telegram from Western Union arrived congratulating the Superior Movement on becoming a part of the Motown stable. We had finally made it, or so we thought.

We told our families and friends that we were signed with the famed Motown Records. After a few weeks we hadn't heard from the record company and had our manager call WBMX to speak to the president of the station, who revealed that he had no idea what he was talking about. It was the first time that he had ever heard of the plot and that the woman whom he hadn't seen in years was not related to him. Lucky for Tyrone, the agreement with her became null and void.

Our hearts were broken and we didn't know how to tell our friends and family that it was all a hoax. By the time we did, it had taken a lot out of us. None of us wanted to rehearse or perform. I started hanging out with friends from my job, and Tyrone, with his friends from the neighborhood. Calvin did what he always did: go from one girl's house to the other, and eventually started to do drugs as did some of the others in the group. Billy was the only one who never indulged. Later, Gregory Spears took Calvin's place and joined the group.

Gun Violence Rears Its Head

During some of our performances, we experienced increasing gun violence. One incident happened downtown at a summerfest in Grant Park; another shooting happened at a nightclub on 87th Ashland on the South Side, and one occurred in our own neighborhood when we were preparing to do a concert in the back lot of Marcy Center at 15th and Springfield. The lot and street were packed with people ready to see us perform. When we started singing, gunshots rang out and people started screaming and running. None of our band members were hurt or shot, which proved God's faithfulness to me because of the prayers of our mothers and people of faith who had been covering us with prayer without our even knowing it, as scripture exhorts us: *"Rejoice always, pray continually, give thanks in all circumstances; for this is God's will for you in Christ Jesus" (1 Thessalonians 5:16-18) NIV.*

Meeting My Wife Antoinette

I met my wife Antoinette while performing at "The Copper Box," a club located on the south side of Chicago. I believe it was truly faith that brought us together. Superior Movement was entering the club during the midst of a fashion show in which she was a model. I couldn't keep my eyes off of her. She was modeling a sheer white dress, and before the night was over, I'd asked her for her phone number.

The next day I called her, and we set a date to go out on my birthday, which was coming up. As we began to get acquainted, she told me how she had chosen me even before I had met her. Her manager had given her a poster of the group, she took it home with her, and began telling her sisters and cousins that she was going to bring me home. A week later, I was at her house. I fell in love with her not only because of how she looked on the runway, but because she confessed to me that she was a Christian. She reminded me a lot of my mother, and eventually I was hooked. For our first date, we went downtown to see the movie "Superman," and we ate at the famous Ronny's Steakhouse.

At the time, Antoinette was working at a toy store in Water Tower Place. I would take the train downtown to her job and ride the bus home with her after work. We were together so much that people thought we were sister and brother. As time went on, she was experiencing difficulties at home and asked if she could move in with me. She was living in Englewood at the time, and my mother, my brother Randy, and I lived in an apartment at 12th and Springfield. I didn't know how to ask my mother, fearing that she would say no, but she loved Antoinette as much as I did, and agreed that she could live with us. Although we knew that we were living in sin at the time, we thought it was OK because everyone else was doing it.

Antoinette and I did everything together. We would go to concerts, plays, hang out, and play cards. When she later found a job at Oak Brook Center, and I was working at Hillside Academy as a teacher's assistant and bus driver, we would go to bars during happy hours.

Life Post-High School

*"Whether you turn to the right or to the left, your ears will
hear a voice behind you, saying, "This is the way; walk in it."*
—Isaiah 30:21 NIV

After graduating high school, I had to make the decision
whether to go away for college, or stay at home and go to
college in the city. Following the words of scripture above, I prayed
about it and decided to attend Northeastern Illinois University
on the north side of Chicago. I had the chance to play football
for two colleges out of state, but turned them down because I was
more interested in the success of Superior Movement. I believed
that there was something special about the group, and that God
was going to help us succeed.

When I went to try out for the football team at Northeastern,
I had the revelation that I couldn't afford to get hurt if I were
going to pursue a singing career. When I entered the gym for
my try-out, spread out before me were huge 6 foot and over,
300-pound white boys! They reminded me of the high school
team we played against and had gotten beaten 56-0. Then and
there, I made the crucial decision that my football playing days
were over.

When basketball season began, I thought that I might play on Northeastern's basketball team. Once again, I had another revelation: I wasn't going to play basketball, either. The guys trying out were tall and quick. I was 5'11" when I played forward in high school. Now that I was in college, I was expected to play guard because of my size. The problem was that I wasn't a very good ball handler and I knew that my chances of making the team were slim, so I gave up playing that sport as well.

Enrolling at Northeastern

At Northeastern, I signed up for only music courses. I wanted to develop my voice and learn how to play the piano. I didn't realize that I had to take certain prerequisites until my advisor, Dr. Ronald Combs, chairman of the music department, informed me. He gave me a brochure that listed the classes I needed to take if I planned to major in music. I needed to take 18 credit hours of voice and learn a second instrument along with the other requirements. I ended up joining the school's concert choir and the opera workshop team. I performed in two Gilbert & Sullivan operettas, "The Gondoliers," and "Patience." In both performances I had to wear sixteenth-century costumes. I enjoyed it, but I didn't see myself pursuing an operatic career.

At Northeastern, I couldn't understand why I was struggling so hard with my music classes. In grammar school and in high school, I got all A's in all of my music classes. But in college, I was getting C's and D's. All the other students were getting A's and B's, and none of them seemed to be struggling. It was then brought to my attention that they had better music teachers in their former schools. They were taught the fundamentals of music and about classical composers, but we inner city students didn't have that luxury. Our teachers were usually young inexperienced white females who had just graduated college. We lacked the books and school supplies that my classmates took for granted. I made a commitment to myself that I was going to learn everything I could about music and take it back to my community. But I had some catching up to do. What I was learning, I had never been taught by my music teachers in elementary school or high school. I learned how to really read music. I learned how to build scales and construct chords. I learned music theory and the history of music—things that weren't taught in the public schools in my neighborhood.

Joining the Gospel Choir

I also joined Northeastern's gospel choir. It was the closest thing to God for me at the time since I wasn't involved in a local church. I didn't have a clear understanding of who Jesus was at that time in my life, but because of growing up in church and hearing choirs sing of Him, and my mother and her peers calling on Him, I gave Him respect and honored anyone who followed Him.

The gospel choir held spring concerts and sang at various churches on Sunday evenings. Marylyn Whitehead led the choir and a fellow by the name of Tim McGee was music director. Marylyn was also a counselor for the program "Project Success," which helped inner city students to adjust and succeed in college. She offered me a chance to join, and I did, thankful that she'd welcomed me into the program, because, without it, I wouldn't have done so well while I was at Northeastern. The program offered tutoring, which I needed to pass several of my classes. It also allowed me to discuss problems I had with staff or other students. I was proud to have been a part of Project Success. With the population of Northeastern at that time being 75 percent white, it was good having somewhere to go where people could relate to what I was going through.

Although we may not realize it at the time, God places people in our lives to help us fulfill our purpose in life. Some people are there for a season, some for several seasons, and some for our entire lives. By exercising our faith and knowing that God is guiding our lives, we become aware of those that He has placed in our paths as embodied in the scripture, *"Do not neglect to show hospitality to strangers, for by so doing some people have shown hospitality to angels without knowing it" (Hebrews 13:2) NIV.*

Being in the gospel choir helped me to continue to walk by faith, even though I wasn't a member of a church. I still had talks with God about being my Father, and I always thanked Him for helping me out of situations that I know I couldn't have gotten out by myself.

My Summer Job at the U.S. Post Office

Every year during summer break, I would apply for a job at the downtown Chicago post office, and every summer I would get hired. Without fail, when I would fill out the application, they'd send me to work at the post office in the community where I lived. I couldn't believe the favor that I was receiving.

During the summer, most regular mail carriers were on vacation, and I would fill in for them. I was what they called an "NTE," meaning that I would work for 98 days during the summer. The challenge for me was that when the regular carriers would show me how to set up their routes, it was different than the way they normally set theirs up. This meant that I had to find out how to set up the route on my own.

One day as I was delivering mail by the route that they had prescribed for me, I had to deliver mail halfway down the block, and then cross the street and start on the other side, deliver it halfway down the block, and cross over and do the other side of the street. It made no sense to me because all I had to do was deliver mail on one side of the street, and when I finished, deliver mail on the other side. It became obvious to me that it was done so that I wouldn't finish ahead of schedule.

Most of the time when I finished my route, I would go home and take a nap. Then at about 2:30 p.m., I would return to the post office and punch out. Most of the mail carriers upon finishing their route, would go to a bar around the corner from the post office. Some would shoot pool while others would play darts. One carrier would come to work drunk, and everybody at the station knew it. Even the people on his route knew when he was drunk, but he made sure that they got their mail. I worked for five straight summers, and most of the time my terms would be extended to 196 days.

Part of my territory was in Cicero, a town that was very racist in the 1970s. When I had to deliver mail there, I had to be on guard because I didn't feel safe. One day as I was delivering mail, several young white teenagers began calling me out of my name.

"Hey Nigger, Hey Nigger!"

I continued to deliver the mail as they followed me down the street. Thankfully, an elderly couple heard them and made them leave me alone.

On another occasion while delivering mail there, a small dog began to bark at me. I didn't see where it came from, but it kept following me, barking at me. I never had the chance to use the mace that I carried, so I wanted to try it out. When the dog ran up to me, I got into my stance and began spraying the mace. The dog ran home and its owner came out. She didn't say anything, but I'm sure she knew that the dog had gotten sprayed. I felt badly but I wanted the dog to leave me alone and I got the chance to test the mace out.

One of my supervisors, seeing how diligent I was at my job, gave me a couple of his old uniforms that he no longer needed. Although I can't remember his name, he was like a role model to me because he was educated and cared about doing his job. The post office ran smoothly under his leadership. If I had to choose any other job besides the one I currently hold, it would be working as a mail carrier.

The Sting of Discrimination

After attending Northeastern for five years, it was time for me to make another serious decision in my life. I went to Dr. Combs and told him that I was ready to graduate. I had followed the curriculum guide and completed the 18 credit hours of voice that I needed to complete the requirements for my degree. Dr. Combs told me that I wasn't ready to graduate and said that I needed to take two more voice classes at the 300 level. I maintained that the guide didn't say that, only that I needed 18 credit hours of voice to graduate. For the very first time in my life I felt that I was being discriminated against. I didn't know who to turn to and thought it was just how the system was. It led to my dropping out before graduation. I dropped out not only because of that situation, but also because my fiancée was pregnant, and I knew that it was my responsibility to take care of my child, requiring me to get a job.

My First Encounters with Racism

"Woe to those who make unjust laws, to those who issue oppressive decrees, to deprive the poor of their rights and withhold justice from the oppressed of my people." —Isaiah 10:1-2a NIV

I kept wondering whether I was really a victim of racism when I had the confrontation with Dr. Combs. I had no one to talk to about it, and the struggle was locked within me. I knew that God wanted to use me to show whites that all blacks weren't alike. This belief was revealed to me as a little boy of eight years of age during the riots of 1968, after Rev. Dr. Martin Luther King, Jr., was assassinated. Before the riots, the community where I lived had many stores. There were shoe stores and clothing stores up and down Madison Street and Pulaski Road.

One day, as I was playing in front of my house, I saw a young white couple running to their car and four black boys trying to turn the small car over. The image has never left my memory. It was the first time in my life that I had seen a human being of another race being violated. My mother called me into the house soon afterwards, but what I had seen has remained with me until this day. God told me then that He was going to use me to let white people know that all blacks weren't alike. I didn't hear an audible voice, but I knew it was what I was supposed to do.

As children, we didn't come into contact with white people unless at school, at the doctor's office, shopping at a store they owned, or unless they were police officers. Speaking of police officers, we did have policemen visit our school occasionally. They were called "Officer Friendly," and they would encourage us not to get involved with drugs and gangs. Thus, we never got the chance to know them on a personal level. I found out early in life that some whites, not all of them, have subliminal feelings hidden deep inside them. It's not their fault. Perhaps it was rooted in their great-great grandparents who may have been slave-owners and while they may appear to like you, deep down there lies something that will cause them turn against you.

Victimized by Racial Profiling

During the mid-1980s in my neighborhood it was common for the police to stop you anytime that they wanted to. One day as Tyrone and I were driving home from rehearsal, my son Antonio who was about six years old at the time, was with us, and we were stopped by the police. I asked the policemen why they stopped us, and they replied that there had been a robbery in the neighborhood. They ordered us to step out of the car, place our hands atop the van, and spread our legs. They subjected my son to this treatment as well.

I was humiliated and embarrassed. Although they ended up letting us go, the stain remains with me to this day. I believe that because of this incident, my son has harbored a hatred for the police ever since. I don't know if he has overcome it by now or not, but I remember a time when I was driving my car with my wife and him in the back seat. As I passed a squad car, we both noticed how Antonio stared the police car down with a hard look. He and many other youths in the community didn't like the policemen who patrolled our neighborhood because they would stop them, planting drugs and guns on them, making it hard for the neighborhood young people to trust them.

A decade after my encounter with the Chicago police, my son Antonio got a job with the CTA after we had protested that the city wasn't hiring residents from our community. He was 18 years old at the time he took the test and passed. Having saved enough to buy himself a car, he was driving home from work one night when the police pulled him over. Antoinette's intuition kicked in, and she sensed something was wrong. We later found out that Antonio had been arrested and put in jail. I went to post bond for him, and before I had handed over the money, I asked what he was being charged with. They replied that he had a gun in the car. Right then I knew that he was a victim of racial profiling and, unbelieving, I kept saying to myself, "a gun!"

Antoinette couldn't believe it either. We asked Antonio if the gun was his, and he said that it wasn't. We knew that one of the policemen had planted the gun in his car, which they had impounded and which someone had broken into, stripping it of its accessories.

Coach Gordon had gotten a Christian lawyer friend of his Dan Radakovich, to represent Antonio and his case. At the hearing several white policemen were in attendance to support their co-workers. Lawndale Christian Community Church had been very supportive of us, and we filled up half of the courtroom.

We were fortunate because so many of our young black men don't get the support they need when going through the justice system. They listen to their friends, are assigned a public defender, and usually plead guilty even when they are innocent. We, on the other hand, had the church behind us, a Christian lawyer, and God Himself. *"He has shown you, O mortal, what is good. And what does the LORD require of you? To act justly and to love mercy and to walk humbly with your God"* (Micah 6:8) NIV.

Anne Gordon of Lawndale Christian Community Church served as a character witness on my son's behalf. She knew our family very well and knew as well that Antonio wasn't involved with any gangs, drugs, and wouldn't carry a gun. The lawyer representing us put the policeman on the spot because he hadn't read Antonio his Miranda Rights. Antonio was acquitted, and all charges against him were dropped.

A Second Son Is Victimized

My middle son Antwane had a similar experience. At one o'clock one morning when he hadn't come home, and we didn't know where he was, Antoinette woke me up and told me to go and find him. I didn't know where to begin to look for him, so I drove around the neighborhood several times when the Holy Spirit told me to check the police station. I went there only to learn that he was in the lock up. "What is he doing in lock up?" I asked myself.

First, they told me that they weren't allowed to tell me why he was there, but a sergeant came out and told me that they had found a small amount of marijuana in his car. It wasn't enough to charge him, but the officer made the decision to bring him in anyway. I found out later from Antwane that the officer saw that he had never been arrested before and told him that because he didn't have a record, he was bringing him in to establish one. The case was thrown out, but it makes me wonder just how many young black boys have to endure this kind of mistreatment from the police.

My Tenure at Hillside Academy

I'd never heard of Hillside Academy, a special education school in the western suburbs, until I saw an ad in the newspaper for teachers' assistants. I applied for the job, and on my very first day I almost quit. Although I had applied for a teacher's assistant position, they had me installing "no parking" signs up and down the streets. My female boss told me to put the signs up, only to tell me to take them down an hour later. When I did as I was told, she told me to put them back up again. It made me wonder whether she was testing my willingness to follow orders.

The Bible tells us that, *"Whatever you do, work at it with all your heart, as working for the Lord, not for human masters"* *(Colossians 3:23) NIV.* I was trying to live by this scripture; however, had she told me to take them down one more time, I would have walked off the job. Despite this, I ended up staying there for seven and a half years.

A lot of unusual things went on at this school. When a student got out of control, our job was to have the student go to the time-out room, a small, cushioned closet with a tiny window. Students would be told twice to go to timeout, and if they refused, we would physically escort them to the room. If the student put up a struggle, we would have to proceed with a take-down, a procedure in which we would sit with the student in a sitting position, roll him or her over onto their stomach and lay on top of them. One of us would be on the top of the student's body, and the other person would lay across the student's legs.

I remember the time when we had a situation with Bill, a big, stocky white student who wore a leather jacket and black clothing most of the time, and smelled as though he had been smoking weed. Mrs. Taylor, the head teacher of the class, informed me that Bill needed a time out. We both approached him, and I asked him to go to time out with us. He refused and began to call me out of my name. I asked him a second time, and he continued calling me names. Then suddenly, and with a rush, I said, "Mrs. Taylor, Bill needs hands on!" so I grabbed him, took him down, and Mrs. Taylor followed my lead. We were both lying on top of him while he struggled to get up. He finally calmed down and walked to the time-out room with us. I was kind of nervous because Bill was much bigger than me, and I knew that I had to move quickly because I couldn't let him get the upper hand.

In another situation at Hillside Academy, I had to take down a student named Sam. At the time, a piece of my hair weave was coming loose. Why I had let Tyrone convince me to get the hair weave in the first place, I don't know. Anyway, I was about to walk Sam to the time-out room when he tried to snatch away from me.

Immediately, I pushed him to the ground and my weave flopped across my face. I was embarrassed as I quickly pushed the hair back on top of my head, not knowing whether the other students saw it or not.

The Friday before, as I was dropping my last student off in Evergreen Park, he rubbed me on the head and said, "See you later, Mr. Ratliff." His eyes got wider as he said, "Mr. Ratliff, you have a toupee!"

I told him that I didn't. The entire weekend, I kept thinking about this student telling the whole school that I was wearing a toupee. Fortunately, he didn't reveal my secret, and the following week I had my sister-in-law Jackie to take it out.

Earning Trust on the Job

Over time, the administration at Hillside Academy began to trust me, and asked if I had other friends that might be interested in working there. By the time I left, I had helped ten of my neighborhood friends get jobs there.

Hillside was also my first exposure to gay people. Walking up the stairs one day, I caught one of the male staff members, Barry, staring at me. I found out later that he was gay. I also learned that he had relatives that lived in my neighborhood, and I would see him on my block off and on and would speak to him. Barry had a best friend, Reggie, who also worked at Hillside Academy. Both were gay and lived together in Oak Park. In time, I got to know them. They never approached me in a way that made me feel uncomfortable, and I was glad to be their friend as long as the relationship stayed that way. Sadly, both died of AIDS while I was working there.

There were also a couple of teachers who worked at Hillside who would sometimes come to work high. Even the students knew it because they would be seen nodding at their desks. I walked into their classrooms several times and had to wake them up. I was reluctant to report them because I knew that they would lose their jobs, but I knew that eventually they would get caught by one of our supervisors.

Two more coworkers at Hillside, Austin and Donnie, were excellent athletes. Austin could have played professional basketball, and Donnie played semi-pro football and basketball. I enjoyed playing ball with them during our free time. The students never challenged Austin because he was a military veteran and they knew it. He had better control of his class than any other teacher at the school.

Donnie and I co-coached the school's basketball teams. One weekend after one of the games, Donnie asked me to accompany him to his brother's house. When I went, I noticed that his brother had a stolen school vehicle at his house. I didn't say anything because I didn't know for sure that it had been stolen, and I didn't want to get him in trouble. I didn't hang around people who committed crimes growing up, so after seeing the stolen van, I kept it to myself. I didn't even mention my suspicion to Donnie, although I'm sure he knew that I knew.

Profiled Once Again

As part of my job, I would also drive the school's van to pick up students. As an incentive, I'd earn money if I could drive the whole year without getting a ticket. At the close of one school year when I was picking students up who lived in Brookfield, I was about to make a turn with a semi-trailer truck on my tail. I wasn't about to miss my turn, so I made the turn and heard the squeal of the brakes of the semi-trailer behind me. I continued on my route picking up the rest of the students. All of a sudden, a police car stopped me and the patrolman told me that I had caused the driver of the semi to lock his wheels. I explained that I was making a turn with the semi-trailer driver too close to me. The policeman instructed me to follow him to where the semi-trailer truck was stopped. I had to do what he said because Romans 13:1 says that we must obey those who are in authority.

When I got back to where the incident occurred, he and

the truck driver were on a first-name basis, so I knew I was in for it. I ended up getting two tickets from the Brookfield police. When I told my boss about the tickets, he told me I had to go to court and that they would withhold my incentive money until everything got cleared up. Eventually, the tickets were thrown out, but I never did get that incentive money.

A Turning Point in My Life

"I have told you these things, so that in me you may have peace. In this world you will have trouble. But take heart! I have overcome the world." —John 16:33 NIV

In 1989, I was unjustly convicted of a crime that I didn't commit. I hadn't seen my friend Donnie in three years when I ran into him at a restaurant where we exchanged phone numbers. About two weeks later, he showed up at my house saying that it was his birthday, and he brought along some beer and marijuana. As we were indulging, Antoinette complained that the car note needed to be paid after which she left the room. Donnie asked if I needed to borrow some money, and I asked him for $500 dollars until I got paid. He then asked if that was all I needed, and I upped it to $1,000, not knowing whether he really had it or not. He took me to his car and gave me ten one-hundred-dollar bills! I promised him that I would give him something toward it every time I got paid.

Now I had a new friend to hang out with, so I began hanging out with Donnie and staying out all night. I had stopped coming home at night and I stopped calling to let Antoinette know where I was. It became clear to me that Satan had used Donnie to get to me. Even though I wasn't in the church at the time, I knew that what I was doing was wrong.

Donnie paid for concert tickets, tickets to sports events, and when we went to bars, he would pick up the tab. He even paid for limo rides every now and then. I have to admit, I was amazed at the things I saw in the underworld. We would go to people's houses, where they would play cards all night. I had never seen so much money on a card table at one time.

I saw people betting fifteen to twenty thousand dollars. They were lawyers, doctors, aldermen, and policemen at the table playing cards. I would sit on the couch and fall asleep. *"For I envied the arrogant when I saw the prosperity of the wicked" (Psalm 73:3) NIV.*

At about five or six a.m., Donnie would wake me up. I could tell if he had won or not by the way he acted. If he won, he would say with a smile on his face, "Come on man, let's get out of here!", and we would go out for breakfast. If he had lost, he would say, "Wake up man; time to go!" Then he would take me home.

Caught Up in a Drug Bust

One day after work while I was headed home, I noticed Donnie's van outside of one of his friend's apartments. I knew he was there because about a week before, we were watching college basketball games during "March Madness." I remembered that Donnie wanted me to pick up some tickets to the upcoming O'Jays concert, so I decided to stop and get the money from him. As I rang the bell, I was buzzed in, and I heard someone say, "Donnie it's for you!"

As I proceeded up the stairs, Donnie was on his way down to meet me. When he approached me, he handed me the keys to his van and told me to drive. I thought to myself that when we got into the van, he would tell me where we were going, but when I had gotten into the van, he was getting into a car parked directly across the street. Looking into the car, I could see that he was arguing with a white female.

At first, I thought it was one of his friends until he got out of the car and into the van. He pulled out a Walgreen's plastic bag and told me to give it to her. I told him that I didn't want to get involved in his quarrel, but he was persistent and finally persuaded me to give it to her. I didn't ask what was in the bag; nor did I try to look inside it. All I wanted was to get home because I knew that Tyrone was at my house waiting for me.

As I approached the driver's side of the car, the woman motioned me to come around to the passenger side. Everything was happening so fast that I wasn't thinking straight. I thought that the reason she wanted me to get into the car was that she wanted me to tell Donnie something. Instead, she opened up the bag that I had given her and then she suddenly pulled out a handful of money and began to count it. I told her that I didn't know what was going on, but was going to get Donnie.

As I opened the car door, I was met with five policemen with guns drawn to my head. They threw me on the ground and handcuffed me. I tried to explain to them that they were making a mistake and that I didn't know what was going on, but they weren't listening to anything I said. Then they put me in a squad car and took me to the Bellwood police station where I was put in a room with Donnie, who assured me that he would tell them that I had nothing to do with what had happened. In fact, he had given them a written statement that I had nothing to do with it, but I was still kept in lock up.

Taken to the Cook County Jail

The next day we were transported to the Cook County Jail, where we would have a bond hearing. When they started processing me, they took me to the basement, and my eyes were opened. I couldn't believe what I was seeing. Never in my life have I seen so many black men at one time being taken to jail. It reminded me of what I had seen and read about slavery. As I was being processed, I saw more than a hundred naked men being transported one way, another hundred-plus naked men being transported another, and a third group of about the same number being taken in another direction.

We had all been forced to strip in the cold basement of the County Jail as they prodded us like cattle. The officers who worked in the basement were at least 6'5" and 250 pounds or more. They wore black leather gloves with the fingers cut out, and looked as mean as ever, talking to us as if they were slave masters, daring us to say anything to them. I remember clearly at one point an officer telling us to move with the flow and not to turn around. All of a sudden, I heard someone being slapped extremely hard.

"Didn't I tell your black ass not to turn around?" the officer yelled. After that, not a soul made a sound or attempted to turn his head. I was intimidated as I'm sure many of us were. Being naked and told what to do was a humbling experience that I wouldn't wish on anyone.

I had thought that since Donnie had told them that I had nothing to do with what had happened, that they would let me go. As I approached the bench for my arraignment, I noticed that the judge was a black female. I thought to myself, "OK, we got a sister on the bench, and she knows how unjust the system is." I just knew that once she heard how I got involved in this mess, she would definitely discharge me. To my surprise, she didn't let me go. I was being charged for delivery of a controlled substance—eight ounces of cocaine was in the bag that I had handed to the undercover agent. She set the bail at $100,000!

I couldn't believe what I was hearing! Did she really say $100,000? I found out later that I had to pay ten percent of that to get out on bail, but ten thousand dollars is still a lot of money. My job only paid about $11,000 a year, so I had to come up with $10,000 in one day. Naturally, I began praying. I told God that if He got me out of this mess, I would start going back to church and serve Him. I hadn't been to church in years.

A Way Out of No Way

After praying every day while I was locked up, God answered my prayer. What had happened was that Donnie had gotten out the next day. Antoinette called his house every hour on the hour, telling him, "You got Stanley into this; you get him out." He ended up paying six thousand dollars and my mother put the remaining four thousand dollars on her credit card.

Deep down inside, I knew that this had to be God because I didn't have the money. Somehow the Lord made a way for them to come up with it to get me out of jail. I memorialized this miracle in one of the songs I've written from my Voices of Lawndale CD, "A Way Out of No Way."

After being out on bond for about a week, the Holy Spirit kept reminding me of the prayer that I prayed to God, bringing Coach Gordon to mind. He was now a pastor at a church in my community. I went to see him and explained that I was in a little trouble, but would soon be out of it once I got through with court. He prayed for me and then invited me to attend church the following Sunday, and I took him up on his invitation.

When I got there, I saw two men that I knew in high school and played football with. All three of us were going through major trials in our lives: One was dealing with a troubled marriage; the other was caught up in drugs, and I, of course, was confronting an issue with the law. But James 1:2-4 NIV says: *"Consider it pure joy, my brothers and sisters, whenever you face trials of many kinds, because you know that the testing of your faith produces perseverance. Let perseverance finish its work so that you may be mature and complete, not lacking anything."*

After the service, Coach Gordon asked if we would consider attending a Bible study with him on Wednesday mornings. We all agreed to come at 6:30 a.m. before work. It was like déjà vu because when we were in high school, we attended Bible study with him after football practice.

The Church and the CCDA Come to My Aid
The year 1989 was also the year that the Christian Community Development Association (CCDA) held its very first conference in Chicago. I attended it because Lawndale Christian Community

Church was the host. Coach Gordon asked me to help, and I did. I met some wonderful people from Dayton, Ohio, and we hung out that weekend. I told them about the situation that I was going through, and they prayed for me and encouraged me.

At one of the services John Perkins, a world known Christian advocate for equal rights and justice and one of the founders of the Christian Development Association, had an altar call and prayed over me. I was desperate to hear from the Lord that He would deliver me from this situation, but it didn't happen the way I wanted it to; it happened the way God wanted it to: *"For my thoughts are not your thoughts, neither are your ways my ways, declares the Lord. As the heavens are higher than the earth, so are my ways higher than your ways, and my thoughts than your thoughts"* (Isaiah 55:8-9) NIV.

Whenever I went to court, I would report back to the Bible study group that my case was continued. This went on for several months. The scenario was the same each time I went to court. The judge would call both Donnie and I up together, and he would say the case will be continued until the next month. For seven months this went on.

Finally, one day Donnie was called up by himself. He had plea bargained and was given ten years. They allowed him to go home for thirty days, after which he would have to turn himself in. That same day they called me up to the bench and asked if I wanted a bench trial or a jury trial. Because I didn't know better, I chose to have a jury trial. I thought that if civilized people heard how I was involved, they would find me innocent. Besides, I didn't want the judge to decide my fate because every time I went to court, he would be reading a newspaper and drinking coffee.

Found Guilty of Delivering Drugs

The trial had begun, and the state's attorney's opening statement and closing statement were the same: "Ladies and gentlemen of the jury, that young man sitting over there is Stanley Ratliff. He's responsible for bringing drugs from Colombia to Chicago."

I thought to myself that they won't believe him because he was lying. I hadn't been out of Chicago in twenty years. How could he say that about me? Nevertheless, they believed him. His job was to get the jury to find me guilty, no matter what it took.

The undercover agent took the stand, and my lawyer asked her a series of questions: Had she ever seen me prior to the date of this incident? She replied "No." When I got into the car, was there any conversation about drugs or money? Once again she replied, "No." While she was counting the money, did I reach for it? For a third time, she said, "No." Next, my lawyer tried to introduce Donnie's written testimony about my having nothing to do with what had happened.

They then called a sidebar, and the jury wasn't allowed to hear Donnie's statement. They found me guilty of delivering drugs. The other charge against me—the charge of possession of a firearm that had been found in Donnie's van that had been pinned on me was dropped because they couldn't prove that my fingerprints were on it. Before the jury had left the room, my lawyer went over to one of them and asked him how they found me guilty. He replied that I had lied when the state's attorney asked me what we were doing in the house a week before the incident, saying that I had said we were watching football, when it was basketball season.

I was scared, nervous and intimidated when I was on the stand. As I testified, tears ran down my cheeks and into my mouth. I was sobbing uncontrollably, getting more confused and discombobulated. I didn't remember whether it was football or basketball we were watching since it had been nine months earlier. All I knew was that it was a game, and that's what I should have said. Besides, it had been almost a year since the incident had occurred. Nevertheless, I was now a convicted felon and I was taken into custody. Antoinette and my best friend Tyrone were both in court as I was taken away. Both, like me, were in awe and cried in disbelief. The next time they would see me would be at my sentencing hearing. Psalm 142 NLT describes my plea and state of mind at the time: *"...Hear my cry, for I am very low. Save me from those who try to hurt me. For they are too strong for me. Bring me out of prison so that I can thank you. The godly will rejoice with me for all of your help."*

My Sentencing Hearing

It had been about a month since my court hearing. While I was back in the lock up waiting to go before the judge, I was in a cage, or "bullpen," they called it. Ten other people were there with me waiting to go before the judge. Each of us would discuss our situations, and someone in the group would say, "Man you can beat this case," or "You'll probably get probation since it's your first offence," or "Your case only carries two to five years."

They really didn't know what they were talking about, but because it was my first time, I believed them. Coincidentally, one of the men in the bullpen with me was one of my former students from Hillside Academy. When he saw me, he said, " Mr. Ratliff, what are you doing here?" I explained to him that the police had set Mr. Murphy (Donnie) up, and, in return, he had set me up.

They called my name to go before the judge. As I looked out in the courtroom, I noticed that it was crowded with people from the Lawndale Christian Community Church. One woman from the church, Tammy Doig, took the stand on my behalf as a character witness. The rest of the members stood up for me so that the judge could see that I had support. He then ordered them all to sit down and went on to say that I had no background in crime and that I seemed to be a model citizen, but unfortunately his hands were tied. He said that because the case carried a mandatory sentence of nine to thirty-five years, he had no other choice but to sentence me to nine and a half years to the state penitentiary. Everyone in the court had teary eyes, including me. As they led me away, I waved goodbye to Antoinette with a broken heart.

Antoinette visited me the next week while I was still locked up at the Cook County Jail. As we were talking through the hole in the glass window, it was very difficult to hear one another. The inmate in the booth next to me had two visitors as well. He was shouting at his girlfriend, and then all of a sudden, he told the young man who had come with her to slap her! I couldn't believe that he actually did it!

Antoinette began to cry, and then told me that she was pregnant. My heart sank because for the first time I realized that I had let her down. Not only was I on my way to prison, but was leaving her alone to raise a baby by herself. I really felt bad, and there was nothing I could do about it. Here I was locked up, and all I could think of was that I'm going to prison. I had never been arrested or locked up in my life, and now, all of a sudden, at the age of thirty-three, I'm a convicted felon. But God has a way of getting our attention, no matter who we think we are. I think about Paul and how he was persecuting Christians. It wasn't called Christianity during biblical times; it was called "The Way." Paul had gotten permission from the high priest to bring anyone who followed Jesus back to Jerusalem and put them in prison. As a result, Jesus stopped him in his tracks on the road to Damascus, and from that point on Paul became a believer and began living his life for Christ.

Entering the Tier at the County Jail

As I entered the tier, everyone was looking and shouting at me. One guy yelled, "Hey, I like those gym shoes!" I kept walking, and to my surprise, a fellow from my neighborhood shouted, "Y'all leave him alone!" He approached me and said, "You're going to be all right. I run this tier." His name was Skip, and although I didn't know him directly, I knew a couple of his brothers. He was a member of the gang, the Vice Lords, one of the largest in North Lawndale. Skip knew that I was a member of the Superior Movement and that I had never been involved in gang life. No one bothered me while I was there, but the only white boy on the tier had been violated by another inmate. I didn't know the details, but the guards ordered everyone out of their cells and into the hallway.

When we got into the hallway, everyone had to stand on their tip toes and press their fingertips against the wall. I was already in jail for something I didn't do, and was being punished for something else that I didn't do. I started crying and praying to God. Afterwards, the white boy pointed at me and told the officer that I had nothing to do with what had happened. By that time, I was really in tears but glad that he had spoken up. I was allowed to go back to my cell, but all the other inmates who were in the hallway ended up going to solitary confinement.

Transferred to Joliet State Prison

I told Antoinette what had happened, and she came to visit me a couple of times at the County Jail before I was transported to Joliet State Prison. When a person gets convicted in the State of Illinois, he is first sent to Joliet State Prison before being transferred to another prison that is farther away. While in Joliet, I ran into Donnie, and he told me that he had thought they would let me go. He also told me to tell Antoinette to send the bail money that he had given her back to his wife.

I thought it was a ridiculous demand from him. My life was in ruins, I didn't know what to do, and it was all because of him. There was absolutely no way I was going to tell my wife to do such a thing. In fact, I found out later that Donnie had asked a friend of his to go to my house and ask Antoinette for the money. Antoinette responded that she wasn't giving him a dime!

Learning the Prison Lingo

Now that I was in prison, I had to learn the lingo. The first term I learned was "chow line." A voice would come over the intercom and say, "Chow line's walking!" meaning that it was time to eat. Whether it was breakfast, lunch, or dinner, whenever you heard it over the loudspeaker, it was time to eat. The first time I heard it, I practically ran because I was so hungry. I was near the front of the line, and all of a sudden, someone began shouting, "Neutrons in the back." I thought he was talking to someone else, but then I realized he was talking to me. I turned around and he pointed at me and said, "Neutrons in the back." I told him I wasn't going anywhere. Then, all of the sudden I heard someone calling my name from the front of the line. It was Trent, who lived on my block. He told me to come to the front of the line. Then he explained to me the jailhouse rule: The Vice Lords are at the front of the line, the Disciples are behind them, the Latin Kings are behind the Disciples, and all Neutrons are in the back of the line. I didn't know it, but Neutrons are the new inmates not affiliated with a gang. But how was I supposed to know it if no had told me?

"Zoo Zoos" and "Wham Whams" were special sweets that the inmates bought during their trips to the commissary. Several inmates gambled in cards games, backgammon, and other games. Because they weren't allowed to have money in their possession, when they would lose, they would go to the commissary window and buy "zoo zoos" and "wham whams" to satisfy their debts.

Another jailhouse term I learned was "shake down," an instance in which the authorities suspected that an inmate or his cellmate were involved in breaking a prison rule such as possessing contraband or some other infraction. The prison guards would conduct a surprise visit to a cell and demand that each inmate vacate it. Then, two or three guards would enter and ransack the cell by turning over the mattresses, emptying out all of the drawers, and emptying the garbage can on the floor. The inmate would be left with the responsibility to clean up the cell and put everything back into place. Fortunately, I had never had to undergo a shake down.

Welcome to the Dixon Correctional Center

"Continue to remember those in prison as if you were together with them in prison, and those who are mistreated as if you yourselves were suffering." —Hebrews 13:3 NIV

About a month later, I was being transported to Dixon Correctional Center in Dixon, Illinois, "Home of Ronald Reagan!" I didn't know it until I saw the big sign as we entered the city on the prison bus. When we got to Dixon, the first place they put us was in the infirmary, where they gave us a physical and a blood test. We were housed four to a room.

One evening, a stocky, tall guy of about 6'4" came in and asked whose name was Stanley. I was surprised because I didn't think anyone knew me there. I raised my hand slowly and said, "I'm Stanley." He said that the minister wanted to see me. I replied, "The minister?" I thought he was talking about the chaplain, but it was "Minister Rico," the leader of the Vice Lords.

When I met him, he asked me if I knew certain persons. Everyone he mentioned were people that I had grown up with and knew from my neighborhood. Some were even friends of mine. Then he told me if I needed anything, to let him know.

As I was walking back to my room, I started talking to God, telling Him, "Lord, I've never been involved with gangs before, and I'm not getting involved with them now. I'm trusting You and only You, so be with me."

I was serious, and can remember that prayer to this day. God heard my prayer as He said in His Word, *"Never will I leave you; never will I forsake you (Hebrews 13:5) NIV.* And it was true. He didn't leave me; nor did He forsake me. He walked with me all the time that I was incarcerated. My thoughts were similar to the prayer of the psalmist David when he wrote: "I cry to you, O Lord; I say, *"You are my refuge, my portion in the land of the living. Listen to my cry, for I am in desperate need; rescue me from those who pursue me, for they are too strong for me. Set me free from my prison, that I may praise your name. Then the righteous will gather about me because of your goodness to me"(Psalm 142:5-7) NIV.*

I began to attend church services on Sundays and Bible studies on Wednesdays. Anytime a special church service was held, I was there. I began to grow as a Christian, and God continued to prove Himself to me that He was real and that He had my back. God said, *"You will seek me, and find me when you seek me with all of your heart"(Jeremiah 29:13) NIV.*

Christian and Gospel Music Become My Lifeline

The yard was where all the prisoners hung out whenever we had free time. We could play basketball, lift weights, buy food at the "Chicken Shack," play cards and dominoes, walk, or jog around the yard. I chose to jog around the yard wearing my headset and listening to gospel music. While jogging, I would wonder how on earth I got myself into this situation. Someone had given me a tape of Twila Paris' "Do I Trust You?" I had never heard of her until I received the tape. Mind you, I grew up on rhythm and blues, and now I was listening only to gospel or Christian music. Up to that point, I had never been interested in listening to a white singer or band. Not that I was biased, I just grew up in an environment where only rhythm and blues were played.

When I would play the Twila Paris song, I could feel God's spirit was in the music, and it helped minister to me while I was incarcerated. Tears would flow from my eyes and down my cheeks as I jogged. At times I couldn't control them, so I just let them flow.

A Chance Reunion with a Neighborhood Friend

After being in the infirmary for a week or so, I was transported to Building 26. As I was walking, I ran into Michael Sweat, a friend from the neighborhood who had graduated from Penn School with me and used to get in trouble often.

"Stan, what are you doing down here?" he asked. I replied that I was asking myself the same question. He knew that I was a member of Superior Movement, so he told me to meet him that night at 6:30 in Building 39, where a couple of bands were practicing. Michael had introduced me to one of the bandleaders, L.A., with whom I became the best of friends. He invited me to join his band.

In time, I confided with L.A. about a problem I was having with Pendleton, my cellmate. Pendleton knew I was a Christian, and that it was my first time in prison. He told me that he was an atheist and at times would curse me out and Jesus, too. Pendleton's actions brought to mind the scripture Psalm 14:1 (NIV): *"The fool says in his heart, "There is no God." They are corrupt, their deeds are vile; there is no one who does good."*

The Holy Spirit would bring to mind the scripture from Deuteronomy 32:35, every time Pendleton would make a negative comment about my faith: *"It is mine to avenge; I will repay. In due time their foot will slip; their day of disaster is near and their doom rushes upon them"* NIV.

Adjusting to Life in Prison

As time went by, I continued to try to adjust to the prison life. It was an unwritten rule of privacy, that if one is occupying a cell with a cellmate, if he puts a towel over the small window of the door, out of respect for the other occupant, the cellmate shouldn't enter. So, when I saw that Pendleton had placed a towel over his window, I wouldn't enter until it was taken down. In the same way, I had expected him to respect me when I put towel over the window.

One afternoon, I had placed a towel over the window so that I could pray. As I began praying, I heard the key turn, the doorknob being twisted, and the door open. It was Pendleton. He had disrespected my privacy and started to laugh. I felt humiliated. I told God that I could not take any more of it and went to the day room just so I could think. L.A. came in and asked what was wrong. I told him what had happened, and he told me not to worry and that he would get me out of the cell.

The next day, he went to talk with an inmate, Tufain, whose cellmate had been taken to solitary confinement because he had broken into the commissary earlier. L.A. told Tufain that I was a Christian and how Pendleton kept taunting me. Tufain agreed for me to move into the cell with him as long as I didn't invite my Christian brothers to conduct Bible study. He considered himself a Muslim and only observed Ramadan, the Islamic holiday that lasts a whole month.

After I moved in with Tufain, he saw that I read my Bible every day, and he decided to buy himself a Koran, which he brought into our cell but never opened to read. He put it on top of the television, where it stayed the entire time I was incarcerated at Dixon.

Even though Tufain wouldn't allow my Christian brothers to enter our cell, it didn't matter to me because I would visit their cells to have Bible study. One inmate I will never forget is a guy named Michael, whom most of us called "Brother Mike." I was amazed by his knowledge of the Bible, which he knew from the Book of Genesis to Revelation! I wanted to be like him, and therefore went to every Bible study class he conducted in his cell.

Despite my enthusiasm, however, I often fell asleep during his class. Like Paul, in his words: *"I want to know Christ—yes, to know the power of his resurrection and the participation in his sufferings, becoming like him in his death" (Philippians 3:10) NIV.*

The Prison Visit: An Exercise in Humiliation

I was fortunate to have visits every other week. If Antoinette weren't visiting me, someone else from my family or the neighborhood would come out to see me and offer encouragement. Among them were members from Lawndale Christian Community Church, in addition to Andrew and Daphne Moore, Donna and Robert Holt, Julie Hill, and Larry and Regina Turner.

Coach came whenever he got the chance despite his frustrated attempts in the face of an uncooperative administration to marry Antoinette and me. Even though I appreciated these visits, I didn't like the preparation procedures that I had to follow in order to receive visitors.

Because we were inmates, the guards would have us to strip naked in a small room. Then, they would have us to bend over and spread our butt cheeks and cough, ostensibly to dislodge any contraband that we might be trying to smuggle out. Afterwards they would force us to open our mouths wide and move our tongue up and down and from side to side. At the end of the humiliating process, we were allowed to dress for the visit. Adding to the indignity, we had to repeat the procedure at the end of the visit.

A Babe in Christ

I was a "babe in Christ" and if Christianity was real, I wanted to know everything I could about it, so I went to every Bible study and attended every Christian church service and every special service that Dixon offered. One group from Prison Fellowship held special seminars twice a year. The title of one of the seminars was "Knowing God." I really wanted to know who God is, and the seminar was a lot of help to me. I received a certificate for completing it as well as other seminars.

The late Chuck Colson, attorney, and former special counsel to President Nixon, who was sentenced to prison for his role in the Watergate scandal, and who had become a "born again" Christian, had founded the ministry, Prison Fellowship. He came to visit Dixon a few times. Once a year, Prison Fellowship presented to the inmates the "Angel Tree Program," where the inmates would apply for their children to receive Christmas gifts on behalf of the program. I was one of the few who took advantage of it. I couldn't believe how blessed my children were to receive gifts that they thought had come from me.

Prison Fellowship would forward the applications to churches and other organizations who would then buy the gifts, making sure that the children would receive them by Christmas. Christ Church of Oak Brook was the church that sponsored the gifts for my children. For two consecutive years, Bill and Nan Barnhart, members of the church, participated in a Bible study group that had agreed to buy gifts, not only for my children, but for Antoinette as well. When I got out of prison, I met them, and since then, they have been part of my extended family. We love them dearly and thank God for allowing our paths to cross.

Once a month, a woman by the name of Mother York, who has since gone home to be with the Lord, also came to conduct Bible study. She was loved by prisoners all over the State of Illinois. Not only did she visit our prison, but she visited almost every prison in Illinois, holding church services and serving hot meals to the inmates. After eating prison food every day, we appreciated when someone on the outside brought us some "real food." Among the foods she would bring were fried chicken, greens, and cornbread. When she came during Thanksgiving and Christmas, she would bring turkey and dressing, greens, and cornbread.

As I reflected on what I planned to do while in prison, I came up with three goals: to get to know God better, to get my college degree, and to teach music in the school. To learn as much about God as possible, I invested a lot of time reading His Word, going to Bible study, and attending church services. I was convinced that if God was real, He knew that I was innocent, and He knew how I got involved with this situation. I also knew that He would get me out as well. I didn't know when or how, but I kept telling everyone that He was going to get me out. I had hope, and I had faith in a God whom I have never seen, but always knew existed, always knew cared, and always knew had a plan for my life. By accomplishing the first goal, I believed that the remaining two would fall into place: *"And we know that in all things God works for the good of those who love him, who have been called according to his purpose." (Romans 8:28) NIV.*

There were the nay-sayers and unbelievers who were taunting me and trying to cause me to doubt, but I stood on my faith and the Word of God. One particular nay-sayer was a guy named Drew, whose cousin Danny was one of my Christian brothers. Every chance Drew got to tease me and my Christian brothers about our faith in Jesus, he did. He would call us fake Christians and say that we were a gang. All the time while I was in prison, I had to listen to Drew's criticism.

"Jailhouse Religion"

While some called my conversion "jailhouse religion," I knew that the true and living God was present in the prison where I was, and His church was alive an active. I couldn't agree more with the Apostle Paul when he wrote: *"I have been crucified with Christ and I no longer live, but Christ lives in me. The life I now live in the body, I live by faith in the Son of God, who loved me and gave himself for me" (Galatians 2:20) NIV.*

More than half of the Christian men who were incarcerated and were involved in the church in Dixon are out of prison and are now leaders in the churches throughout the Chicago area; some are even ministers and pastors! To God be the glory!

Joining the Gospel Choir at Dixon

Another aspect of my Christian growth was joining the gospel choir while I was in prison. During my first visit to the church, before joining the choir, I saw a young man leading worship and I thought to myself, "I can do that!"

About three weeks later, the man had gone home, and the chaplain asked if I would mind leading the music for the worship service. It was a no-brainer for me because I was already gung-ho for Jesus. Anything that I could do to enhance the Kingdom I was open to. In prison, I had found myself a church home and had gotten a little Bible study under my belt, so it was important that I participate using my spiritual gifts to enhance the Body of Christ in the local church. According to scripture, all the parts of the body come together to become the functioning church that God has called it to be: *"So in Christ we, though many, form one body, and each member belongs to all the others" (Romans 12:5) NIV.*

Completing My Degree in Prison

"But the wisdom that comes from heaven is first of all pure; then peace-loving, considerate, submissive, full of mercy and good fruit, impartial and sincere." —James 3:17 NIV

My spirituality came first, then the opportunity to go to school while I was in prison. Two schools were represented on the prison campus, Sauk Valley Community College and Roosevelt University. Before being incarcerated, I had 120 credit hours from Northeastern Illinois University. I had been a music major and I wanted so much to get my degree. I met with an advisor from Roosevelt University and explained my situation. He said that Roosevelt University would accept 64 of the 120 credit hours that I had earned from Northeastern University, and all I had to do was complete an additional 18 credit hours to satisfy the requirements for my degree. I was excited because, upon completing the 18 credit hours, I would receive a degree in general studies. I told myself, any kind of degree was better than no degree at all, so I began Roosevelt University's program.

I enrolled in a paralegal class with Pendleton, who was known to be a jailhouse lawyer and helped a few inmates with their appeals. At the end of the paralegal class, I got an "A," and Pendleton got a "B." He couldn't believe that I had gotten a better grade than he. Nor could I. But God had given me wisdom and understanding to get through the class. I think of Daniel and the three Hebrew boys, and how God gave them wisdom after denying themselves the king's food, fasting, and drinking only water. After three years, they were smarter than anyone from the Babylonian kingdom.

After a year and a half and taking all the required classes, I ended up back in the academic advisor's office. I told him that I had completed all the classes and the 18 credit hours and was ready to receive my degree in general studies.

"Mr. Johnson, I have some bad news for you," he said.

I replied that my name is "Ratliff," not "Johnson," and he said, "I have worse news for you. We won't be able to accept all of the 64 credit hours from Northeastern University; we can only accept 46 of them. I told him that he'd told me that he would accept the 64 hours I had earned there. He said that he was sorry, but that there was nothing he could do about it.

I was discouraged, and my heart was hurting, so I went to talk to the chaplain, Henry Bauma, and explained everything to him. All of the men who attended church services loved him. He was a spiritual counselor as well as a friend. After crying and sharing my plight with the chaplain, he said, "Stanley, let's pray."

Afterwards, he picked up the phone and called Northeastern University on my behalf. "I am the chaplain here at Dixon Correctional Center," he said, "and I have a young man in my office who has 120 credit hours from Northeastern University and 18 credit hours from Roosevelt University. How can we work together and help him to get his degree?"

The person on the line asked for my name, and he replied, "Stanley Ratliff." Looking up my transcript, he told Chaplain Bauma that I didn't need any more credits and that I had earned them already! All I needed to do was take the English Competency Test and I would receive my Bachelor's Degree in Music.

Two weeks later, they sent the English Competency Exam to the English Department of Roosevelt University, I took it, and in another three weeks, they mailed me my bachelor's degree in music on behalf of Northeastern Illinois University! Praise God! It was truly a miracle, calling to my mind when Jesus looked at his disciples and said: *"With man this is impossible, but not with God; all things are possible with God"(Mark 10:27) NIV.*

Teaching Music in Prison

At Dixon Correctional Center, I had the choice of either working in the kitchen or the library. As we lined up one by one and entered the room before making our choices, everyone who preceded me exited saying they were going to be working in the kitchen. When I entered to make my choice, I was told to have a seat at the desk. The person interviewing me said that the only job that was available was working in the kitchen. "The kitchen!" I exclaimed. "I don't want to work in the kitchen!"

During the interview, a man entering the room and overhearing our conversation, said that a job in the library was available if I wanted it. I said, "Sure, why not?" The other inmates were amazed at how I ended up getting the job in the library and not the kitchen. I knew that it was the favor of God, who gives us favor when our hearts are turned towards Him: *"Then you will win favor and a good name in the sight of God and man" (Proverbs 3:4) NIV.*

After a month of my working in the library, L.A., my bandleader friend, had lost his job as a music instructor. Before he left, he had told his boss about me and about my abilities.

He asked if I would mind taking over his spot, and I told him "No." At the same time, my name came up to work in the industry building, making Illinois license plates and working for other companies that contracted with the Illinois prison system. Inmates who worked in the industry building got paid more than those in any of the other jobs in the prison. I had to decide about what I was going to do, so I began praying about it. I believed that God wanted me to be there more for the inmates than for myself and that He wanted me to show them love and to teach them music, so I took the job teaching music: *"Do nothing out of selfish ambition or vain conceit. Rather, in humility value others above yourselves, not looking to your own interests but each of you to the interests of others" (Philippians 2:3-4) NIV.*

When I started teaching, my first student was Leo, a fifty-year-old Italian who was a heavy smoker and reeked of tobacco. He also was a loner who lacked friends. He had been labeled as having a learning disability and thus was unable to enroll in regular classes. As I began teaching him to play the piano, he grew interested in it more and more. For the first time in Leo's life while in prison he had a friend and was learning something new. Leo never missed a day of class and soon began to play songs on the piano.

Before long, I was teaching music and piano to more than sixty men. They appreciated me taking the time to work with them, which helped them to pass time while we were incarcerated. Smiley, an African American who was about sixty-five years of age, was another inmate whom I taught to play the piano. He had his wife bring him a Casio piano so he could practice. He took his piano lessons seriously until the guards found him dead in his cell from a drug overdose. It broke my heart because I loved Smiley and the dedication he brought to my music classes.

A Yearning Desire for Release from Prison

All the while that I was teaching music and going to school, I yearned to get out of prison. I applied for an appeal and was denied. I didn't want to approach him, but I asked Pendleton to draw up the papers to get me a court appearance, and they denied it as well. I was eager to make something happen, though, so I prayed, but I didn't wait to hear from God. Instead, I asked for a non-believer's help. Waiting on God and trusting Him takes an act of faith. As humans, we want things to happen according to our timing and not God's timing: *"Wait for the LORD; be strong and take heart and wait for the LORD" (Psalm 27:14) NIV.*

Finally, I told God that I wasn't going to fight Him anymore. I would let go, and "let God." I told God that if He wanted me to do all of my time here, then let His will be done. As soon as I did, He gave me a comforting peace that had eluded me: *"And the peace of God, which transcends all understanding, will guard your hearts and your minds in Christ Jesus" (Philippians 4:7) NIV*.

All I knew was that I was content, and all He wanted for me was to focus on Him. God had protected me, took care of my family, and gave me joy in the middle of my trial. Only He could have done such a thing!

A week later, I received papers in the mail announcing that I was to have a clemency hearing on December 10, 1991. I knew I hadn't filled out any papers, but I found out later that Antoinette and my brother-in-law Richard had filed for a clemency hearing on my behalf. I wasn't allowed to attend the hearing but my wife, Coach Gordon, and my other brother in-law William were there. I had been told that after all the other cases had been presented to the judge prior to my case, the state's attorney would rebut them, saying that none of the inmates should be released from prison for any number of reasons. When my case was presented, the state's attorney didn't object, stating that whatever the pastor said was correct.

Afterwards, he told Coach Gordon that he had reviewed my case and that I never should have been sent to prison in the first place. He added that he knew several people on the review board and that he would inform them that I had nothing to do with what had happened and that I shouldn't remain in prison. When I heard that, I leapt for joy, telling everyone that God was going to get me out. I had been telling them that for the longest, but I was then more confident than ever. I told them that I would be out before New Year's Day, thinking that December 10th through the 31st should be enough time for them to process the paperwork to get me released. To my surprise, it didn't work out that way.

An Answered Prayer

The date was December 31, 1991. It was a quarter to midnight, and I had just completed Bible study in a friend's cell. As I approached the day room where everyone was watching a Chicago Bulls play-off game that had gone into overtime, all of a sudden Drew shouted, "Stan, you said God's going to get you out of here by New Year's. You got fifteen minutes!"

Everyone was laughing at me. I walked through the day room with my head down, feeling embarrassed. Then I had a talk with God, and He said, "My timing is not your timing." I kept on praying and believing God, and on March 6, 1992, the clemency was granted! It happened this way:

Every Friday I would call the Lawndale Christian Community Church and talk to Coach Gordon, asking how the church was going. I'd always tell him how I was doing as well. Sometimes, when he wasn't there, I'd speak to the church's secretary Willette, and would sometimes sing a song that I had written. On one particular day, Coach Gordon answered the phone with the words "Congratulations, Stanley. The governor has granted you clemency!"

Stunned by the news, I replied that it was great, but that I hadn't heard anything about the governor granting me clemency. He then told me to hang up and call him back in fifteen minutes. He was going to confirm it with my mother. I couldn't wait fifteen minutes, so I called him back in five. He had talked to my mother and said that the governor's office called and said that, yes, that Governor Edgar's office had granted me clemency, and that he was on his way to pick me up. I could hear the excitement in Coach's voice.

When I hung up, I ran through the prison hall telling everyone, "I told you! I told you!" The expressions on some of their faces showed their disbelief, while others wondered aloud "How?" I recalled the words of the gospel song, "He's an On-

Time God": "He may not come when you want Him, but He'll be there right on time!"

They didn't believe me when I first told them that I would be released, and now they saw first-hand how God had made a way out of no way. I made sure that I went by Drew's cell to tell him the good news. He looked bewildered and dumbfounded. Then I went to my cell to tell my cellmate Tufain. The towel was on the door's window, and I knew that I shouldn't have entered, but this was good news!

I opened the door, and Tufain was sitting on the toilet smoking a cigarette. I pointed to him and said," I told you God was going to get me out of here!" The news had spread throughout the prison that I had been granted clemency. Guys kept coming up to me asking me if they could have my shoes, my clothes, and any other personal effects that I would be leaving behind at Dixon. At the time a scripture from Psalms came to mind: *"… and call on me in the day of trouble; I will deliver you, and you will honor me" (Psalms 50:1) NIV.*

My Release from Dixon

When Coach Gordon arrived with his son Austin, he told the guards that I had been granted clemency and that he had come to take me home. The prison guards replied that I wasn't going anywhere because they hadn't heard anything from the governor's office. Coach insisted that they call Springfield for verification. After they called, the clemency papers were faxed over.

Coach told me that he'd take me anywhere I wanted to eat and asked where I wanted to go.

"If you want ribs, I'll take you to Carson's Ribs. Anywhere you want to go, Stanley, we can go." I told him to take me to McDonalds. "McDonald's?" he asked. I said, "Yep, Mickey D's. That's where I want to go!"

After the trip to McDonald's, we headed home, and when I got to my house, there was a big gathering for me. Family and friends were all on the front porch and sidewalk in front of my house. When I opened the car door, I heard my son Antonio running toward me screaming, "My daddy, my daddy, my daddy is home!" He leapt into my arms and gave me a big hug. You could tell he was as happy as I was.

After the celebration was over, it was time for Antoinette and me to spend time together. It had been two and a half years since I'd held her in my arms the way I wanted to. However, I wanted to do things God's way according to Proverbs: *"He who finds a wife finds what is good and receives favor from the LORD" (Proverbs 18:22) NIV.*

We had lived in sin for thirteen years, so Coach Gordon advised us not to sleep together again until we were husband and wife. Antoinette lived in an apartment directly across the street from the church, and I continued to live with my mother for a week. Our goal was to get married the following Sunday during church services.

When Sunday came, the church was packed. When it was time, everybody was waiting for Antoinette, so Coach Gordon had to leave the church to go across the street to get her. When they arrived, we finally began the wedding service. Marcus, the ten-year-old son of one of my friend's, sang "You Are So Beautiful" as Antoinette, my bride, came down the aisle.

All were impressed by Marcus's powerful voice. When he dropped to his knees, the expression on Coach's face showed that he was unaware of the boy's talent. For our honeymoon, we were gifted a two-day stay at a five-star hotel. We celebrated by opening up and reading the many cards of well-wishers, amazed by the monetary gifts that we had been blessed with.

Life Post-Incarceration

"What no eye has seen, what no ear has heard, and what no human mind has conceived—the things God has prepared for those who love him." —1 Corinthians 2:9 NIV

After my release from prison, I needed to start making money so that I could support my family. At the time, two former football players from Farragut: Andrew Moore, and Dwayne Hurley, reached out to me. Both attended Lawndale Christian Community Church. Andrew owned his own cable company and hired me to work with him on several projects. I was no good at manual work, but I appreciated Andrew for looking out after me, and I did give it a try.

For the most part, all I had to do was feed him the cable lines while he installed them. Dwayne, who has since died, worked downtown as a parking lot attendant and introduced me to one of his customers who owned a furniture refinishing company. When he hired me, my job was to stain furniture. It was a good paying job, but it wasn't my cup of tea, either.

Several members from Lawndale Christian Community Church reached out to me and would either invite my family over for dinner, or if they had a job that needed to be done around the house, would hire me. I had dinner at the homes of Andy and Debbie Krumsieg, Dale and Reese, and many others. Lisa and Dave Wilcoxen, who had bought a home on my block also invited me to help them remove old wallpaper with a blow dryer. It was a meaningful time in my life because God was bringing new friends into it.

About a month while I was out of prison, my sister Lynette, who was also a teacher at Gage Park High School, asked me to help her with starting a gospel choir at the school. I did, and the choir was truly amazing. Many of the students were in the choir at their home churches and had outstanding voices. We began singing at various schools and community events. We even performed at a Black History program at the Lawndale Christian Community Church. Because the choir was doing so well, the National Council of Negro Women presented me with an award plaque for appreciation of what I was doing in the community with these young students.

In 1993, two of my sons were attending Chicago Westside Christian School and somehow my wife got me to teach the children's choir there. It was a good thing because every little cent that I made would help around the house. The choir was doing well until I had to quit because I had to cope with managing my diabetes and high blood pressure. However I was asked to join the school's board. I didn't really know what I was supposed to do by being on the board, but it was a learning experience. One thing we did accomplish while I was on this board was to establish the new school building that they are in now. I was a part of the planning and fundraising event. This was indeed my introduction to the not-for-profit world. I thank God for the opportunity to serve and meet some amazing people who truly care about the children living in Lawndale.

Building New Homes in North Lawndale

Before I came home from prison, Antoinette and six other families had been meeting once or twice a month making plans to build their own homes from the ground up in North Lawndale at 1830 and 1838 S. Springfield. I joined them, and after a year or so, we broke ground and started building. All the other families involved in the project were headed by single mothers except for Craig Nash and the architect Perry Bigelow, the mastermind behind the project. Perry collaborated with Lawndale Christian Community Church in the endeavor, and we all signed an agreement to help build each other's homes.

As the process got under way, arguments broke out because the members of the cooperative weren't showing up to work on the homes. After much struggle, we finally completed what we had started. We built seven individual homes and a common house, and the Ujima Condominium Association was established.

Craig handled the business aspect of the association until he moved out after his daughter Pheanna was struck and killed in an accident involving a semi-truck. As she was standing on the corner near her school, Wright Junior College, a semi-trailer turned the corner and hit and killed her. It was the first death in our housing complex and was followed years later by a homeowner who died of cancer. These deaths brought our small community closer together.

A New Role as Association Manager

I ended up replacing Craig managing the complex and had to make sure that the insurance premiums were paid, that the grass was cut in the summer, and the snow removed in the winter. I didn't mind taking on the responsibilities until the unit owners stopped paying their association fees, which were only forty dollars a month at the time.

To ensure that the insurance was kept up, I even footed the bill at times. In spite of this, one of the unit owners accused me of stealing money. She had no proof of it, and was unaware that other owners weren't paying their fees. It turned out that the very person who had made the accusation was the one who wasn't paying hers.

Antoinette persuaded me to give up the position and let someone else deal with the headache, but when I did, our insurance lapsed, and no one took the responsibility to cut the grass or remove the snow, so I made it my business to see that both were done even though I had given up managing the association. After all, I couldn't allow what God has given us to go to waste. I wanted people to see that it was only because of Him that we were able to build the homes.

We were proud of our accomplishment, and we had started it all by faith and prayer. We continued to pray as we worked, and God helped us to meet our goal. We were the first to build new homes in our community in thirty years. No developers would risk it because it was a predominantly black neighborhood.

After our homes were built, other developers started coming into the neighborhood to build. I had always wanted to put up a sign that read, "Because of God, these homes were built." I have not been able to do so, but it remains a goal, nevertheless, since after nearly 30 years, we're still here. The main thing is that we had our faith and we try to help each other whenever we can. We are still a small community within a larger community: *"By this everyone will know that you are my disciples, if you have love for one another"(John 13:35) NIV.*

The Lawndale College Opportunity Program

The Lawndale Christian Development Corporation (LCDC) is a ministry of the Lawndale Christian Community Church, which has provided countless numbers of apartments and affordable homes to the residents of the Lawndale community. LCDC also had a component ministry, the "Lawndale College Opportunity Program," which selected eighth-grade students from several elementary schools in Lawndale. We mentored them throughout high school, and upon completing the program, the church would award them scholarship money for college. I enjoyed being a coordinator for the program, being with the kids, and taking them to visit various colleges and to college football games.

Many of them are now grown and most have started their own families. In fact, one of them introduced her daughter Tae Tae, who was involved in the music education program of Celestial Ministries that I founded, and later went on to earn her bachelor's degree. I praise God because most of my former LCOP students are doing really well. Candice Halbert went on to earn a bachelor's degree and is now a scientist and has a son. Christopher Bunch is now a teacher with the Chicago Public School system. Kweisi Oliver has his own mechanic shop and is always working on the community residents' cars. Another LCOP former student, Jackie Morris, is a nurse practitioner who was on the front lines during the COVID-19 pandemic that hit the Lawndale community hard.

Involvement in Lawndale Christian Community Church

By then, I had become a full-time staff member of Lawndale Christian Community Church when another responsibility was placed upon my shoulders. I was recruited to lead the church in worship on Sundays and to play the piano for the choir. Pretty soon, I was as busy as ever working for the church, a trap that many church staffers fall into.

I was practically never at home, and I didn't know how to balance my time between work and my family responsibilities. This became a frequent source of conflict between Antoinette and me because I was rarely home to spend time with her and the boys. According to her, it was work, work, and work. To address the situation, Coach Gordon gave me Thursdays off so that I could spend the day with my family, and it worked for a while, until Antoinette got a job working for the clinic at Lawndale Christian Health Center.

As part of the church staff, my job was to set up the chairs on Saturdays for Sunday's service, act as a part-time director of the gym, and work with the church development department. My supervisor, Richard Townsell, at the Lawndale Christian

Development Corporation, had assigned me to take care of one of the church-owned buildings, cutting the grass and cleaning the hallways. When I performed these duties, I would do them as if I were doing it unto the Lord. I loved the job because it gave me a chance to work, and at the same time, talk to the Lord, with Colossians 3:23 NIV foremost in my mind: *"Whatever you do, work at it with all of your heart, as working for the Lord, not for human masters."*

Recording My First CD

While working as the church's minister of music, God placed on my heart to record a CD with the praise team, my cousins, and several others from the Lawndale Community. I didn't know exactly what I was doing, or how it would turn out, but the first thing I did was to gather up all of the songs that I had written in prison. In the process, God would "download" other songs into my spirit, and I would write them down. I would then call my cousin Michael to tell him what I wanted to do. He connected me with a friend, Tony Brown, who went under the stage name "Downtown Tony Brown." As we began working together, I marveled at how he was able to lay down the tracks to my lyrics.

I would sing or either play a tune for him, and he would take it and develop it so that I would have a complete song. I would then seek out people from the neighborhood, the praise team, or one of my cousins to sing lead. This process took several months until finally I had all of my songs on one CD, "Choose Christ," by Stanley Ratliff and the Voices of Lawndale. We held a release party, and the place was packed. The church was filled with members of the congregation, friends, and family. My only regret about the venture is that the CD wasn't mixed well. Although I thought it was a great effort, after listening to the constructive criticism from other musicians, I came to the realization that it could have been mixed better.

The Seeds of Hope House

Several months had gone by, and I went to visit Coach Gordon in his office. He asked me what I thought God wanted me to do now that I was out of prison. I told him that I had a vison that God wanted me to open a home for men who have been incarcerated and that I'd seen men arrive at prison, serve three months' time, get released, and within a month were right back. I'd also seen men who hadn't received a single visit from family or friends as I had, so I wanted to help those men when they got out. *"In the last days, God says, I will pour out my Spirit on all people. Your sons and daughters will prophesy, your young men will see visions, your old men will dream dreams"(Acts 2:17) NIV.*

He told me that a former wrestler who had also attended Farragut, and whom I'd known for years and who had been struggling with substance abuse, had a similar vision. He suggested that I contact him. When I did, I found out that he was a leader at the rehab center, Victory Outreach. I told him that Coach wanted to talk to both of us, and the following week we met.

For two years, we prayed about starting a men's home, and in 1995, Hope House was established at 3843 W. Ogden Ave. We started out with only four men living in an apartment. A year later, the ministry had grown to fifteen men. The following year, we moved down the street to 3859 W. Ogden Ave, above Lou Malnati's Pizzeria, where a population of thirty men lived. Finally, we moved to the location at 3759 W. Ogden and had fifty men living at Hope House. God was confirming to us that this was what He wanted for the community of North Lawndale.

Founding North Lawndale's Hope House

"But God demonstrates his own love for us in this: While we were still sinners, Christ died for us" —Romans 5:8 NIV

At first, my partner and I experienced conflicts because he wanted to run the ministry like a rehab center similar to Victory Outreach, which he had run previously, and I wanted to run it the way that I thought God wanted me to run it. Eventually, we came to an agreement, and Hope House began to be a beacon of light in the community of North Lawndale, attracting men from all over the City of Chicago as well as nonresidents of the city. I learned that even though these men had been broken, God still wanted to use them: *"There will always be poor people in the land. Therefore I command you to be openhanded toward your fellow Israelites who are poor and needy in your land" (Deuteronomy 15:11) NIV.*

At Hope House, residents took classes in anger management, financial literacy, and relationship building. They also assisted the elderly, patrolled three neighborhood schools, and volunteered their services to people who needed help moving.

Most had accepted Jesus Christ as their Lord and Savior, and God began transforming and restoring them, making them leaders in the community. Because I was a musician, I noticed that many of these men had special gifts and talents. Some were musicians, some could sing and rap, some were songwriters, and others were mechanics.

We started the Hope House Choir and began singing all over the city. Every Sunday we would go to two, sometimes three churches to sing and share our testimonies. It was a sight to see because of the rarity of seeing fifty black men who had been strung out on drugs or released from prison singing God's praises the way we did. People enjoyed listening to us, and we enjoyed performing.

We sang at the Chicago Theater downtown, and were the opening act for the play "Tell Hell I Ain't Coming," starring Clifton Davis. We also sang for the National Baptist Convention at McCormick Place, we appeared on several radio shows, and sung at a number of summer festivals. We were even invited to sing and march through a Swedish Cemetery in celebration of a Swedish Holiday after someone read an article in the paper about us. I have to admit that there was no way we could have done this by ourselves. Besides, we had several coordinators assist us: Darrin Brown, Victor Heard, Wardell Tate, Antoine Allen, and Daryl Saffore. The chemistry we shared made us an effective team.

Now that I had completed my first CD, God was telling me to record another one. For the first one, He had inspired me to write all of the songs and provided a way to record them. Now, He was telling me to put one together for the Hope House residents. I knew it would be a challenge, but praise God, we were able to do it! I would tell the men after an all-nighter at the recording studio that they had to get up for Bible study at 6:00 a.m. They understood the commitment, and God blessed our endeavor by enabling us to record the CD.

I had written most of the songs, but two of them were written by Felton Burkett, a resident of Hope House, and two were traditional songs. I gave the CD back to God and told Him that He could use it wherever and however He wanted to. As a result, it has been heard around the world: *Then I will ever sing in praise of your name and fulfill my vows day after day* (Psalm 61:8) NIV.

Profiles of 29 Hope House Alumni

To enter the ranks of the Hope House Alumni, a resident had to complete nine months in the program, after which time he had the choice to either move to the transition house, Nehemiah House, or get his own apartment. In order for him to be admitted to Nehemiah House, he had to have a secure job because he was required to pay rent. Many of these men have gone on to live with their families, or in some cases, have ended up owning their own homes. Several are now living productive lives and are leaders in the North Lawndale community. Identified here are 29 men with their brief personal testimonies of the challenges that brought them to Hope House and how they were able to overcome them.

Daryl Wicker. Also known as "Big D," Daryl came to Hope House straight out of prison. When the sheriff brought him in, he was shackled in handcuffs at his wrists and ankles. Now, he works two full-time jobs and helps out with the ministry.

John Raggs. John, an electrician by trade, has been through Hope House several times. After each time, he would relapse. Finally, he took Christ seriously, and now is growing spiritually and owns his own business. Whenever I have an electrical issue at my home or at the ministry, I call John, and he always takes care of it.

Jimmy Wayne. Jimmy came to Hope House after being fired from his job for assaulting one of his co-workers. A former semi-pro boxer, his hands are registered, so he could go to jail for fighting anyone who is not a professional boxer. Jimmy was hooked on heroin when he came to Hope House. I explained to him when

I noticed that he had a package of cigarettes in his shirt pocket, that smoking was not allowed in Hope House, after which he asked if he could smoke his last two. I told him that he could, and afterwards he entered Hope House and completed our nine-month program. He returned to work at The *Chicago Sun-Times* and volunteered as a substance abuse counselor at the Haymarket recovery home.

Robert Anderson. Robert abused drugs when he came to Hope House. After completing the program, he stayed at the Nehemiah House for two years and then got his own home. He gained custody of his children and now is a certified drug counselor and has a license to work in security.

Eric Coffee. Eric completed the nine-month program at Hope House and founded his own transportation company, "Errand Boy," starting out transporting people from church and then eventually transporting them throughout the community of North Lawndale. He now owns a fleet of vans and is currently working out of O'Hare and Midway Airports.

Eddie Sanders. Eddie, also known as "Code Red," completed the Hope House program and is now the main cook at Lou Malnati's Pizzeria in North Lawndale. He has been on the staff there for more than 20 years and is doing very well.

Marvin Rowe. Marvin not only had a drug problem when he came to Hope House, but he had a problem with women as well. While he was living in the Nehemiah House, he got involved with a woman who abused drugs. It took several of us to convince him that she was no good for him until she got help for her addiction. Once, when she was angry at Marvin, she came to Nehemiah House and caused a lot of havoc, forcing us to call the police. Marvin came to his senses soon afterwards, broke up with her, and is now doing well.

Felton Burkett. Felton was a musician who also had a drug problem. When he arrived at Hope House, I recruited him to play the drums for the praise team and I also co-wrote one of the songs on the Hope House CD with him. One of his original songs has also been recorded on the CD. A professional painter, he ended up going to a truck driving school after leaving Hope House and now has a commercial driver's license. Today, he owns his own home and continues to drive trucks across the United States.

Harvey Ross. Harvey led most of the songs on the Hope House CD and has been clean for more than fifteen years. As of this writing, both Harvey and Felton are at work on another CD.

Stan Logwood. Stan was homeless, and his pastor sent him to Hope House. He needed to complete the program twice before he was finally able to get on the right track. He realized that he couldn't fake it. Either he was going to allow Jesus to be the Lord of his life, or he was going to remain in the rut that he was in. When he finally started trusting Jesus wholeheartedly, he was able to see the difference it made in his life. Stan got married and now owns his own home, where he's been living for more than 20 years.

Randy Ratliff. Randy, my brother, abused drugs and has been clean for more than 20 years. Randy had to go through the Hope House program two or three times as well. He now works at the Lawndale Christian Health Center as a supervisor.

Donald Robinson. Donald completed the Hope House program and is another singer whom I could depend on during the Hope House Choir's performances. He also sang in the Lawndale Christian Community Church Choir for a while.

Jimmy Gathers. Jimmy achieved the milestone of being clean and sober for 19 years. Jimmy worked at a tire shop. He currently works in the office of a Cook County Commissioner.

Abdul Qadir Muhammad. Abdul was a young man when he came to Hope House from Philadelphia. He was referred by his Aunt Pat, a friend who asked me if we could try to help him. At the time, I didn't know that he was a devout Muslim. I took him in because our mission statement commits us to help those who struggle with substance abuse and who are released from incarceration. He agreed to follow all of the rules and to attend all Bible study and worship services. As he continued to be a part of our program, I became fond of him because he was a unique individual. Initially, the men complained because I had admitted a Muslim into the program, and on top of that, I allowed him to be the Hope House cook. After several weeks, the men began accepting him because he was a fantastic cook. The men loved every meal that he prepared for them. Now happily married and living in Philadelphia, he has sent me pictures of his family and thanked us for teaching him how to live.

Mike Brown. Mike has been clean of drugs for 20 years. He is married and is currently working at Lou Malnati's Pizzeria.

Bruce Calhoun. Bruce has been a friend for many years, and he helped us to build our home. He came to Hope House and never looked back. He now has his commercial driver's license and is a certified HVAC technician, working for a construction company in North Lawndale.

Carl Johnson. Carl completed the nine-month program at Hope House and married one of its staff members to whom he has been married for more than ten years. He has his own construction company and barbecues for the Hope House men every Fourth of July. He is always looking to help the next man who enters Hope House.

Wardell Tate. Wardell came to Hope House after living a life of drugs and gangs. He has a talent for carpentry that few men have. While other men were building fences in the neighborhood, Wardell was building sheds. He serves on staff at Lawndale Christian Community Church, has his own apartment, and loves teaching the Word of God. A former member of our prison ministry team, he once led Bible study classes at the Cook County Correctional Center.

Anthony Morris. Anthony, a former drug abuser, has been clean from drugs and alcohol for several years. When Antoinette takes families to visit their loved ones in prison downstate, Anthony drives the van and is always there when we need him. He is a blessing for our Angel Tree programs.

Michael Holmes. Michael sang lead in the Hope House Choir and is now recording songs that he has written at Celestial Sounds Studio. A newlywed, he is also his pastor's armor bearer, a member who serves his pastor in any way possible. He acts as a spiritual equivalent to a personal assistant and is employed at Lou Malnati's in North Lawndale as a pizza delivery man.

Tony Jackson. Tony is an alumnus of Hope House who is originally from the South Side. He sang in the Lawndale Community Church Choir as well as the Hope House Choir and served as the cook at Hope House. He is now a leader in his home church.

Tony Howell Bell. Tony has been a driver for Lou Malnati's for more than 20 years. Even though he didn't come through Hope House, Tony is considered as an honorary member. He attended support groups and church services. Tony also works as a pizza delivery man for Lou Malnati's.

Gary Myers. Gary has completed the program at Hope House and lives with his wife Brenda. He is a deacon at the Living Word

Christian Center and assists with the Angel Tree program as well. He also helps with picking toys up for the program.

Andre Williams. Andre, another victim of drug abuse, has been clean for more than 20 years. He lives on the South Side, volunteers for the Angel Tree Program, and performs with us when we do our "Temptations" routine.

Sheldon Clay. Sheldon is the son of the late blues singer Otis Clay. He was the leader of Celestial Ministries drumline, which, had it not been for him, we would have never established. He devoted his time and energy to Hope House for many years and is now on staff as the drummer for Judson Baptist Church.

Anthony James. Anthony completed a work program that landed him a job at O'Hare Airport. Anthony and his wife are always helping us, along with their son, during our annual Angel Tree program. I can call on Anthony anytime, and he will be there for me.

John Howell. John came to Hope House from Peoria, Illinois. After completing the program, he moved into a single-living facility, where he is currently employed. John also assists with our Angel Tree Christmas program.

Billy Ray. Billy is another employee of the Lawndale Christian Health Center and drives the bus for our senior population. He sometimes stops by Celestial Ministries, blowing his horn to let us know he's in the neighborhood.

Nathan Norris. Nathan is the brother of Calvin Ford, a former member of Superior Movement. Nathan owns his own car washing business.

God gets all the credit for the transformation in all of these men's lives. He only used Hope House as an instrument to guide them.

Living Testimonies

During Thanksgiving, the Hope House alumni brothers host a big breakfast at Lou Malnati's Pizzeria for the residents, where they would be acknowledged for continuing to do well. Occasionally, we get together to sing at the funerals of people whom Hope House has recognized as being was instrumental in their lives. There are a number of living testimonies in the North Lawndale community whom those who lack a spiritual eye might overlook. What has kept these men clean and sober and not examples of recidivism is the Word of God. When you are filled with it, there's no turning back. Once you are in His hand, it's hard to pluck you out. In Jesus' words: *"I give them eternal life, and they shall never perish; no one will snatch them out of my hand" (John 10:28) NIV.*

Hope House Is Not for Everyone

Hope House is a good place for men who have been struggling with substance abuse and for ex-inmates, but it's not for everyone. A close friend, Jeffery Ward, who was heavily into drugs and really needed help, didn't think Hope House was the place for him. Knowing that he couldn't succeed at Hope House, he ended up going to a halfway house, Delancey Street, in California. The non-religious-based program is more hard core in its approach than Hope House.

Losing a Gifted Hope House Alumnus and Friend

When Darryl Saffore first came to Hope House, his jaw was wired, and everything he ate had to be processed in a blender. In spite of this, Darryl did everything that was required of him as a Hope House resident.

After he completed the program, he became a coordinator and staff musician for Lawndale Christian Community Church. Because he was a phenomenal pianist, we nicknamed him "Keys." He and I worked very well together, both at Hope House and as independent musicians. I stopped playing the piano because I recognized immediately that he was more gifted than me. We collaborated on the music for the church as well as on music for the Hope House Men's Choir.

Darryl would allow me to lead, and then he would follow, and was my go-to guy when we encountered a musical challenge. Eventually, he decided to pursue a master's degree in music at Northern Theological Seminary. Upon completing it, he went on to get his doctoral degree and became an associate pastor at Lawndale Christian Community Church. Because of his desire to achieve, he inspired a number of others in the community and church to go back to school as well, helping me complete my first year in seminary and assisting me with technological issues I encountered in the process.

Not only was Darryl concerned about the men of Hope House, but his concern extended to many people in his congregation. Hope House was especially amazed at his transformation when he married his wife Julie.

In 2016, I came home to see an ambulance parked outside of our housing complex and was told that it was for Darryl. When I reached the bedroom where he was lying in bed, Coach Gordon was there praying over him, hoping that God would resuscitate him, but it was to no avail. To this day, I cherish his memory.

The Hope House Fence Builders

Another friend and co-worker, Floyd Towner, developed a relationship with a fence builder from Tennessee whose company erects fences throughout the United States. He agreed to train the men of Hope House to build wrought iron fences. The men caught on quickly, calling themselves "Hope Fences."

I took them to the bank every payday, standing in line while they cashed their checks. I ensured that they gave 30 percent of their wages back to Hope House, and I deposited the rest into a savings account in their names. This practice worked out so well that before they left Hope House, they had accumulated three to four thousand dollars in their savings account. After a while, several of them started their own fence company and, as of this writing, are doing extremely well.

Mid-Life Blessings

"You will be blessed when you come in and blessed when you go out." —Deuteronomy 28:6 NIV

Antoinette and I were in our forties when she suffered from persistent abdominal pains. She was administered a variety of medicines, including prednisone, and it seemed like every other day we were headed to the hospital for either the pain or her flare-ups from asthma. This went on for at least five months.

One day, she asked one of her friends who worked at a clinic to administer her a pregnancy test, and the result came up positive. When she asked her to do it a second time, the results were conclusive. She came home and broke the news to me. I was bewildered. When we told our sons Antwane and Antonio about it, they couldn't believe it either. I thought that we were through having children, but four months later, our son Andrew was born. Yes, God definitely has a sense of humor.

The Kingdom Men and Women at the church held a baby shower for us with the men marching around in a circle singing the "Father Abraham" song. We received several gifts: diapers, toys, food, and clothing that we definitely needed at that stage in our lives.

My mother and aunt helped babysit Andrew while we worked. As of this writing, Andrew is 17, weighs 180 pounds, stands 6'3," and plays basketball for St. Joseph High School in Westchester. When we attend his games, we are usually the oldest couple there, but we get a thrill seeing our once little boy develop into a handsome young godly man.

Andrew attended private grammar school and high schools, his tuition paid by special friends. No way could we have afforded to send him to these schools without God placing it on their hearts to act so kindly. He will be attending the University of Illinois at Chicago in the Fall of 2021.

A Trip Abroad to Romania

Christ Church of Oak Brook, with which we were affiliated, had decided to sponsor a mission basketball team from the Chicago area to go to Timisoara, Romania, and chose several youths from their church and from the North Lawndale Community. Bill and Nan Barnhart spearheaded the mission trip. They asked me to accompany them so that I could teach music at the basketball camp, but I coached and taught the fundamentals of basketball as well. The girls' team I coached won first place in the girls basketball tournament.

While in Romania, we visited Debra's House, an orphanage for battered young girls. We also visited a youth detention center for boys, most of whom couldn't speak English. They understood the game of basketball and knew who Jesus was after our sessions. While there, we ate at McDonald's every day because it was the only place where we could get American food. Other times we'd eat at a Romanian restaurant, which was a great experience for my son Antwane and I because we had never been out of the country before. Since the trip, we've been to Romania five more times.

Some nights when the boys were asleep, Kirk Johnson and I would tour the city on foot. I felt safe being with Kirk because of his experience traveling while in the military. He and I lived in the same neighborhood, went to the same church, and our families knew each other, but we had never had the kinds of deep conversations that we had while we were in Romania, where we talked about how church members judged him because he had issues with drugs and didn't always do things the way they wanted him to. Because of this, he insulated himself by appearing to be hard and unapproachable, a defense that he let down once I got to know him. We also engaged in many conversations about his service in the armed forces and his own walk with God.

Kirk was highly intelligent and we had many things in common. I also found out that when I played football at Farragut, I had played against him when he attended Austin High School, and I bragged about our team beating his. In return, he would brag about his team playing at Soldier Field when my team didn't.

A few years after our trip to Romania, Kirk died in a house fire set by a young man seeking revenge against a woman with whom he had a dispute. Kirk lived on the third floor of the building in which she lived, was asleep when the fire broke out, and was unable to escape.

Jim Brost one of the chaperones from Christ Church of Oak Brook, was another person with whom I engaged in conversations while in Romania. He and I would stay up late at night discussing worship songs and our families. A humble man, Jim was a delightful companion to have on the trip.

My Nomination for the Jefferson Award

In 2006, Antoinette submitted my name for consideration for the Jefferson Award, the highest public service award that is given to those in public service. Oprah Winfrey, Lin Swanson, and George H. W. Bush are among the celebrities who have previously received the award. Of 3,000 applicants, only five are chosen to receive the prestigious award in Chicago.

On the application, Antoinette cited all of my contributions to the community of North Lawndale: I was leading Hope House, a half-way house for ex-offenders; teaching music to children, and visiting prisons singing and sharing my testimony.

Marvis Frazier, the son of the late boxer Joe Frazier, was a spokesman for Prison Fellowship, and on a prison tour accompanying Marvis, a spokeswoman for WMAQ TV's Channel 5, called to inform me that I had been nominated to receive the National Jefferson Award. Although I didn't know exactly what it was, I was honored to have been chosen.

After I received the news, I told Antoinette, and we began celebrating and telling everyone we knew. The awards ceremony was to be held in a week's time, and the following Monday Antoinette and I were out shopping for blue shoes to coordinate with my blue suit. Suddenly the phone rang, and it was one of the leaders of my church, Lawndale Community Church, who had complained that a staff member had a problem with my receiving this award.

I handed the phone to Antoinette, who told him that she was upset that he would share such news. After all, she was the one who had taken it upon herself to fill out the application on my behalf. The spokeswoman at WMAQ TV said that another member of the church had called her to complain also. She revealed that complaints from detractors happen all the time and that if everything that Antoinette said that I did in the application was true, that I had nothing to worry about and everything would be all right. And it was. *"He is the one you praise; he is your God, who performed for you those great and awesome wonders you saw with your own eyes" (Deuteronomy 10:21) NIV.*

On the night of the awards ceremony, my friends, relatives, and church family were in attendance. The Hope House Choir was invited to sing a rendition of "America the Beautiful," which we jazzed up and ended with in a rap, to the audience's delight.

Afterwards, the five winners were announced, and I was among them! We received certificates, a bronze coin with "The Jefferson Award" inscribed on its face, and a $1,000 check to be donated to the charity of our choice. At the end of the ceremony, one of the winners was selected to go to Washington, D.C., to represent Chicago for the national award. By the grace of God, I was chosen, and once again, we celebrated. *"Since ancient times no one has heard, no ear has perceived, no eye has seen any God besides you, who acts on behalf of those who wait for him." (Isaiah 64:4) NIV.*

When it was time for me to go to Washington, I invited Mary Cray, my sixth through eighth-grade teacher as well as a board member of Celestial Ministries, the music and fine arts school I founded; Donnie Grahams, another board member; and my wife Antoinette.

When we arrived in Washington, D.C., we were amazed to see the marching guards and the way in which they had set up the stage for event. Approximately 270 people from around the United States had received the Jefferson Award, and of these people, five received The National Jacqueline Kennedy Onassis Award; I was honored to be chosen as one of the recipients.

The winners from each state represented took a picture with the senator of his or her state. At the time, Barack Obama was the senator of Illinois, and I, as well as Antoinette and Mrs. Cray got a chance to talk to him as well as have our pictures taken with him. Of course, I didn't know who he was at the time, and certainly was unaware that he was thinking about running for president. After he had won the election, I thought, "Wow! I was in the same room with this guy! I talked with him and took pictures with him! Now he's the President of the United States!" What a miracle! *"Now to Him who is able to do immeasurably more than all we ask or imagine, according to his power that is at work within us, to him be glory in the church and in Christ Jesus throughout all generations, for ever and ever! Amen" (Ephesians 3:20-21) NIV.*

My Enrollment at Northern Theological Seminary

"The beginning of wisdom is this; Get wisdom. Though it cost all you have, get understanding."
—Proverbs 4:7 NIV

In 2010, I lost my job at Lawndale Christian Community Church. I knew I would survive the loss because God was directing my life. I thought that I would get another job quickly because I knew so many people, and they knew who I was. I couldn't have been more wrong. I thought either my friends or their supervisors would hire me. Again, I was wrong. In fact, it seemed as if these so-called friends were keeping their distance from me, and all I had was my family and Jesus.

I couldn't collect unemployment compensation because I didn't think I was eligible for it. I thank God that I had a pension that I could draw money from until I could find another job, but eventually I had to withdraw every penny until I had nothing left. Afterwards, all hell broke loose. We couldn't pay the mortgage, we couldn't buy food, and our son Antwane was in college at Northern Illinois University. Despite these setbacks, we never gave up hope. God still provided. Several friends of ours helped us make it through those trying times. And it wasn't our closest friends, but those whom we didn't see every day. They knew that I was no longer working and that my family was struggling. We continued to trust God, and He eventually brought us out.

I can remember when our lights were turned off, and we were sitting in a cold dining room with a huge hole in the floor. All of a sudden, the doorbell rang and Sally Wagonmaker, the lawyer who has been doing pro bono work for our ministry, brought food for us. When she saw that we were sitting in a cold house with no heat or electricity, she started to cry. We consoled her, telling her it would be all right, and that we'd get through it, and we did. *"The eyes of all look to you, and you give them their food at the proper time. You open your hand and satisfy the desires of every living thing"* (Psalm 145:15-16) NIV.

Working at Westside Health Authority

Another time, I had to walk two miles to the hospital for a doctor's appointment because I didn't have the money to take the bus. On the way home, I thought about how we didn't have money to send our son Antwane to buy food. While I was walking and praying with my head lowered, I found three hundred dollars lying by a fence. I praised God and called home to tell Antoinette. She was able to buy food and send money to Antwane.

I continued to trust the Lord and was able to secure a part-time job at Westside Health Authority, an organization that helped ex-offenders get reestablished into the community. Although God had placed me there, I knew that I was there for only a season.

Initially, they had me doing data entry and filing, but later they had me go into the prisons to represent the organization. Despite this added responsibility, I still didn't feel that I was being productive. They then had me to teach music to the children in the after-school program, and while there, I got a call from Karen Walker Freeburg, the assistant dean at Northern Theological Seminary.

I had begun taking classes at the Northern Seminary campus in North Lawndale but stopped, and she called to offer me a scholarship to their Lombard campus. I immediately accepted the offer, and when I arrived on campus, a huge banner had been strung across the office door with the announcement: "Welcome to Northern Seminary, Stanley Ratliff." I was so shocked that I began to cry on the inside. These people didn't know a thing about me, yet I could tell that they loved me enough to provide such a welcome.

My Vulnerabilities Are Exposed

My first class at Northern was a formation class, which was more like a support group for me because we were all vulnerable to each other. I was hurting, confused, and, for the first time, I opened up and shared with others what was going on in my life. We prayed for each other, sharing our individual trials and challenges. Everything that we shared was private and confidential. *"Therefore confess your sins to each other and pray for each other so that you may be healed. The prayer of a righteous person is powerful and effective"* (James 5:16) NIV.

Six of the students in the class I was enrolled in were from the North Lawndale community: Phil Jackson, Terrence Gadsden, Stephanie Jones, James Brooks, Mattie Phillips, and Krista Walthall. I was as excited to see them as I knew they were excited to see me. We would carpool together whenever one of us didn't have a ride to campus and studied together for quizzes.

It was kind of strange because we were all from a poor neighborhood, yet here we are students at a leading seminary in Lombard. We all got along very well, and graduated with either a Master of Divinity degree or a Master's in Christian Ministries degree. By then, I was working part-time and going to school part-time. Although it was very hard on me, my family supported me all the way.

Two Notable Professors at Northern

Of all the classes at Northern, one was avoided: the one taught by Dr. Claude Mariottini. He was the toughest professor at Northern. No matter how hard we tried to avoid taking his class, we eventually had to because he taught the Old Testament, which was a requirement for all students. Dr. Mariottini didn't crack a smile, but after enrolling in his class, I realized that he was one of the best professors at Northern because he took his job seriously, and he wanted all the students to take it just as seriously as he did. We would have to read a couple of chapters, and then take a quiz on the material. After learning what he expected from us, I enjoyed being in his class.

Another professor whom all the students liked was Dr. Scot McKnight, a transferee from another seminary who taught the New Testament. Dr. McKnight was the opposite of Dr. Marriottini. He had a sense of humor and was able to build relationships with his students, whereas Dr. Mariottini was more concerned about us learning the material. As seminarians, we were allowed to miss only two classes a semester, and if something important arose requiring us to miss a class after we had already missed two, Dr. McKnight would give us an excused absence as long as the circumstance was legitimate. Dr. Mariottini, on the other hand, would not.

A Lesson About Setting Boundaries

One time, I brought up in class a situation that I felt guilty about involving a young woman who knew my family and asked if I would take her home. She called while I was on break between classes. I told her that I was in class and that I wouldn't be home until about ten o'clock that night. I assumed that she had gotten someone else to take her, but when I arrived home, there she was standing outside of my house. She asked me to drop her off, and since she only lived less than 10 minutes away, I thought I would. It was cold, late, and I was extremely tired.

As I proceeded to take her home, she asked me to stop at the gas station so that she could get some cash from the ATM machine. I was frustrated, but because of my generous heart, I complied. She got out and went into the gas station, but was taking too long. I felt uncomfortable because I didn't want anyone to see me and her together at that time of night and start thinking the wrong thing. I was praying all the while I was in her presence. *"Rejoice always, pray continually, give thanks in all circumstances; for this is God's will for you in Christ Jesus" (1 Thessalonians 5:16-18) NIV.* I knew Satan was behind this when she finally came out and said that there was a problem with the ATM machine.

As I drove her home, I noticed that we were headed past where I thought she lived. After she told me to go a little farther, she had me pull over, saying that she was staying at the destination, "The Cindy Lyn Motel." When I thought she was going to get out, she asked me to sit and talk to her in front of the motel. I told her that I had to go home to a wife who was waiting for me: *"Do not be misled: Bad company corrupts good character" (1 Corinthians 15:33) NIV.*

All the way home I apologized to God for allowing myself to be set up like I had. Dr. Fleagle told me later that I needed to set boundaries because people would misuse my kindness for weakness. I told her that she was absolutely right and that I would never allow such a situation to happen again.

Interning at Living Word Christian Center

When it came time for my internship. I had no idea where I would be assigned, so I started asking different people for their advice. Antoinette weighed in by saying that I should intern at the church we were attending at the time and of which she was a member, Living Word Christian Center.

We had been searching for a church home that we both could agree upon, and after visiting different churches ourselves, we began visiting the churches of our friends. One Sunday, Antoinette went to visit Living Word with our next-door neighbors Mildred and Mary Porter and came home excited. "Stanley, you need to come and visit this church. I think you will enjoy it," she exclaimed.

The following week, I did visit Living Word, and she was right. I noticed that I knew a lot of people who attended the church. I then listened to the music, the choir, band, and the praise team, all of whom were extraordinary. Finally, I heard the pastor preach, and the subject that he preached on was exactly what I felt about God. I was convinced it was the place we needed to be at that time in our lives.

One of the messages that the pastor delivered that stayed with me and continues to resonate with me today is that God strategically places us in dark places as Christians. I was astonished because I knew he was right. Then I reflected back to when I was in prison and I realized that was what I was there for! I was there to grow in the Lord, yet at the same time serve as a light to those around me. I also reflected on why we started Hope House: It was to bring light to the community and help the men who lived there. *"In the same way, let your light so shine before others, that they may see your good deeds and glorify your Father in heaven" (Matthew 5:16) NIV.*

After the service, Antoinette had a conversation with my cousin Tammy Sykes, who was on staff at Living Word. Tammy introduced me to Dr. Linda Morgan, who led the music department. After talking to her, she told me that she would talk to Pastor Bill Winston to see if I could do my internship there.

When I went to visit the following week, I met her in the sanctuary, which was directly across from Pastor Bill Winston's office. As I waited, I began to get nervous. When Dr. Morgan left Pastor Winston's office carrying some papers, she inquired whether I had a background. I told her, "Yes," that I had been performing music for a very long time. But she wasn't talking about that kind of background. She wanted to know whether I had ever been in prison. I couldn't lie because from the papers she held, I could see that they had already done a background check on me. I told her "Yes," and proceeded to explain how I ended up in prison. She replied that the pastor wouldn't hold it against me because I'd be a living testimony proving that rehabilitation was possible and that I could do my internship at Living Word, praise God. God is so faithful, I exclaimed to myself.

The next step for me was to introduce Dr. Morgan to the person who managed the internship program at Northern Seminary, Dr. Jill Fleagle. Dr. Morgan signed papers to the effect that she would be my immediate supervisor, and the process began. I must say that it was nobody but God who got me through it all. Dr. Morgan understood where I was in life and did whatever it took to help me to succeed. I truly appreciated her because of her kindness and sincerity in helping me. I would not let her or my family down and did everything that was required of me. Dr. Fleagle would attend church service if one of her students were preaching, no matter where it was located. She influenced us to be accountable, to stay healthy, to set boundaries, and to make sure that we were following God's will.

My Involvement in Other Ministries at Living Word

As I continued my internship at The Living Word Christian Center, Dr. Morgan suggested that I participate in the newly formed Jubilee Choir at the church. I took her advice and was introduced to some amazing people. When we sang, I felt an anointing from God that I had never before experienced in my life. At one of the programs where we performed, the entire choir was overtaken by the Holy Spirit, and no one could leave, but I had to pick Antoinette up for the next service. As badly as I wanted to leave, the Holy Spirit wouldn't let me until He was ready for me to leave. When I did, I got into the car and wept, thanking God for the experience.

While at Living Word, I was also a member of its prison ministry, which involved our going to Statesville Prison to conduct service for the inmates on Saturdays. It was a joy to be with them and to serve as God would have us to do.

Antoinette and I attended Bible study at Living Word on Wednesday nights. On one night while at Bible study, we received a call from Antoinette's sister informing me that their mother had died. She had been hospitalized for a week, and we hadn't expected her death. I had to figure out how to tell Antoinette because I knew she wouldn't take it lightly. When I finally told her, a woman elder of the church who knew Antoinette, Denise Carly, was there to console her, not leaving until Antoinette had settled down. It was God's providence that enabled us to be in church at the time with someone by our side. *"God is our refuge and strength, an ever-present help in trouble" (Psalm 46:1) NIV.*

My Involvement in The Faith Alliance Ministry

While I was attending Northern, Antoinette was enrolled in Living Word's School of Ministry. Not long afterwards, we both were ordained ministers and members of the church's Faith Alliance Ministry, an auxiliary headed by the pastor, Dr. Bill Winston, that was a coalition of pastors and ministry leaders from around the world who were trained and supported by Dr. Winston.

Living Word hosts a faith conference every year during the summer, and people from all over the world attend. One year, Dr. Morgan asked if I would help out. Professional artists were on the program to minister, and my job was to pick them up from Midway Airport and take them to their hotels.

I had the pleasure of meeting several well-known recording artists, their band members, and families. Among them were gospel artist Israel Houghton, who recorded such songs as "Lord, I Lift Your Name on High, "God Knows My Name," and "You Are Good," and Adlan Cruz, the world renowned Puerto Rican pianist, and others.

I remember picking Adlan and his family up from Midway Airport, and when we got to the hotel, him noticing that one of his possessions was missing. I sensed that he was looking at me oddly, possibly because I'm black, but neither he nor I said anything. He asked if I would take him back to the airport, to which I complied.

It was a very quiet ride to the airport, and I prayed that he would find what was missing. When we arrived at the airport, we went to the security office, which had the missing article, a small pouch that he had left in the cart at the airport. When we got back in the van, he opened the bag and counted out $15,000. I kept praising God in my spirit because I felt as though it had been my fault, and if it hadn't been retrieved, I would have been to blame, jeopardizing my position at Living Word. *"I sought the LORD, and he answered me; he delivered me from all my fears"* (*Psalm 34:4) NIV.*

The next day, Adlan Cruz told me to invite some of my students from Celestial Ministries to hear him play. I did, and afterwards, he took the time to invite them backstage to talk to them and encourage them, giving his personal testimony. They were happy that they had the opportunity to meet him. He told me that if I ever had a fundraiser for my school, he would be willing to come and offer his services.

Obtaining My M. A. Degree in Christian Ministries

In 2012, I was told that my time was up at Westside Health Authority because the grant money had run out and my services were no longer needed. The founder had retired and installed her son and daughter in oversight positions. I then began to focus solely on school, and in 2014, I graduated from Northern with a Master of Arts Degree in Christian Ministries.

Many friends from the North Lawndale community attended my graduation ceremony, so when I walked across the stage to receive my degree, I had one of the loudest applauses of any graduate. After the ceremony, Antoinette had a party for me, and the whole day was filled with joy. I praise God because, without faith, it could not have happened. *"Being confident of this, that he who began a good work in you will carry it on to completion until the day of Christ Jesus" (Philippians 1:6) NIV.*

A Stint as Music Minister at Judson Baptist Church

"Let us not become weary in doing good, for at the proper time we will reap a harvest if we do not give up." —Galatians 6:9 NIV

A pastor friend called me because he had just been installed as the new pastor of Judson Baptist Church in Oak Park, Illinois. He is also a professor at Moody Bible Institute. I met with him at a restaurant on the south side of Chicago. I agreed to help him with the music at his church. My sister Janice was a member of the church and was also on the praise team.

When I first started working with the singers and the band, everything seemed to flow. I was told that they loved to sing traditional hymns and I made sure that during worship service, one was always on the program. I knew that the congregation was moved by the music because they would always tell me so after service.

The Ginter Family, a musical family who were very talented, assisted me with the music. In particular, three siblings, a brother and two sisters, were standouts. The brother played the piano while the sisters accompanied me on the vocals. We performed well together, and when it was time for the Ginter son to go away to college, and he told me that he would no longer be able to play, I told the pastor that we needed a replacement, unaware that one of the sisters was just as talented. After I heard her play, she stepped into the role seamlessly, and we didn't miss a beat.

One day after service, the pastor pulled me aside and introduced me to a man whom he had handpicked to be the pianist for the choir. "We already have a pianist," I thought, but because he was the pastor, I couldn't argue with him. It was hard for me to tell the pianist we had that she would no longer be able to play for us, but I had to. I felt badly because she was a teen and really loved playing the piano for the church. She said in reply that she understood and immediately began singing vocals again.

Later that week, I had a conversation with her replacement, Joe, and immediately picked up some red flags and warned the pastor about it. He told me to let him worry about the red flags, and I did.

Joe wanted me to write out the chords to each song for him. Before he came, the norm was to give a list of the songs to all of the musicians to learn on their own and be ready for rehearsal on Thursday. We never had a problem because everyone would fulfill their responsibilities and come prepared for rehearsal. Another red flag was that when Joe came to rehearsal, he would play the first song, but he hadn't learned the rest, so we had to show him how the songs went. I could see that he was getting frustrated. He began talking about his accolades and how good he was. Sometimes he would leave before rehearsal ended.

I told the pastor that I didn't think he was going to work out, but he told me that I had to make it happen. I said I'd try. I called and apologized to Joe for making him uncomfortable, which he accepted, asking that I just give him the songs with the chords clearly marked.

Never in my life had I had to work with a person who was as prideful as he was, but I did, mindful of the scripture: *"Pride goes before destruction, a haughty spirit before a fall" (Proverbs 16:18) NIV.*

I humbled myself and asked God to give me the wisdom to work with Joe. After the next rehearsal, the Lord gave me the idea of switching Joe to the organ and returning my original pianist to the piano. It still didn't work because Joe just wasn't used to playing gospel praise music.

Although he was a competent musician, his style of playing wasn't in sync with ours. After the pastor met with us, I thought the issue had been resolved, but it hadn't. Joe missed the next two weeks of worship, and when he came back, he still expected me to write out the chords for all of the songs. I recommended that he go on You Tube and learn the songs like the rest of us did, but he resisted my recommendation. To make matters worse, we sometimes had to change the key to a couple of songs, and it took Joe far too long to learn the songs in the new key.

Having reached my limit, I told the pastor that if things kept going the way that they were, I would have to leave. All during this time, I was experiencing health problems related to diabetes, and by the next Sunday, to my shock, the pastor had replaced me with another worship leader. Mistakenly, I had thought we had a better relationship than that.

When Antoinette and I came to the church service that Sunday, the pastor announced that I had resigned because of my health situation. Antoinette walked out of the service with me close on her heels. I had not resigned; I had only tried to convey to the pastor that the arrangement with his handpicked musician wasn't working out, but he tried to force the issue.

Seeking redress, I wrote a letter to the church elders, who replied that I should have told them about the situation earlier. I told them that I had gone straight to the horse's mouth and told the pastor himself. I understood that it was the end of my experience at Judson Baptist Church. I felt vindicated in my response to the situation after the worship leader who was hired to replace me encountered the same problem with Joe that I had. Eventually, Joe left the church.

Although I had thought that I would be at Judson longer than I had, I came to realize that it was God's will for me to be there only for a season. It turned out to be a blessing in disguise because I could then focus on establishing Celestial Ministries, my dream to share my gift of music to the North Lawndale community. Because I was no longer employed, I had to find a way to help provide for my family. *"The Lord makes firm steps of the one who delights in him; though he may stumble, he will not fall, for the Lord upholds him with his hand" (Psalm 37:23-24) NIV.*

Temporary Setbacks

I decided to go to a temporary agency to earn money to support my family, and although I had sworn that I would never work in a factory again, all of the available temporary jobs were for factory work. After forty years in the work world, I found myself working at a factory again.

Right out of high school, Tyrone, one of the members of Superior Movement, had taken me to a temporary agency for work. We had to report at 6:00 a.m., after which they would drive us to a plant on the north side of Chicago. My job was to put paint bucket handles on buckets and place them back on the conveyor belt. I stood on my feet the entire eight hours. It was terrible! I vowed that I would never, ever do work like that again. Imagine working eight hours a day standing on your feet and only getting a half hour lunch and two fifteen-minute breaks! Tyrone asked me if I wanted to go back the next day. I told him, "No, thank you." He didn't go back either.

Now, forty years later, I had a bachelor's and a master's degree, and yet the only job that I could find was working at a factory. The temporary agency didn't have to drive me to the work site this time because I had my own vehicle. Everywhere I was sent was located in the northern or southern suburbs. The first place was a factory where I had to load and unload barrels onto a semitrailer truck. It was easy work but time-consuming.

After a while, I began to weaken and wasn't able to work as fast as I wanted to. Moreover, I was always very tired when I got home.

I didn't know how much of it I could take, and after a week working there, I was sent to another site in Forest Park, which was closer to home and a much easier job. All I had to do was put together packages at various workstations. I was timed to see how many packages I could assemble by the end of the day. I liked the work because I got along well with my fellow employees, but after a week, I got a call from the agency not to return the next day without telling me why. I reported for work anyway and was met by the foreman, who asked if the temp agency had called to tell me not to report for work. When I told her that I had gotten the message, but thought it was a mistake, she ordered me off the premises as if I had stolen something. She walked me to the front door. As we were walking, I kept asking her what was the problem, and she never answered. All she could say is that I had to leave right then. Suddenly, I remembered that I was an ex-offender.

I had been granted clemency, but the conviction was still on my record. Never before had I felt so humiliated. I started questioning why it was happening to me. All I had wanted to do was to work and provide for my family, but I had come face to face with the reality that this was the life for many other felons who had paid their price to society and were still being treated as criminals. In my heart though, I was confident that, as scripture says, *"The Lord will vindicate me; your love, Lord, endures forever— do not abandon the works of your hands." (Psalm 138:8) NIV.* God has our back, and He will make sure that we are victorious as long as we continue trust Him.

I had reached another turning point in my life. I knew then that I had to get Celestial Ministries up and running so that I could become my own boss. Being a black man with a conviction on your record is a stigma that can severely affect your life. I vowed that I would place my trust in God and Him only. I've seen over the course of my life how fickle people could be when they have control over you. I didn't like it, and I was determined to do something about it.

Founding The Celestial Ministries School of Fine Arts

"Whatever your hand finds to do, do it with all your might,
for in the realm of the dead, where you are going, there is neither
working nor planning nor knowledge nor wisdom."
—*Ecclesiastes 9:10 NIV*

Having been a beneficiary of the Angel Tree program that sponsored Christmas gifts for children of inmates when I was an inmate at Dixon, Antoinette and I decided to implement the program at Lawndale Christian Community Church in 2006 as a means of giving back to the North Lawndale community. This initiative was inspired by Hebrews 13:3 NIV, *"Continue to remember those in prison as if you were together with them in prison, and those who are mistreated as if you yourselves were suffering."*

We started out by inviting to our program 50 children whose parent had been incarcerated. We hosted events at which we put on skits and plays and sang songs accompanied by the Hope House Choir. For refreshments, we served pizza or hot dogs along with soft drinks. Afterwards, we presented them with gifts and toys on behalf of their incarcerated parent. It was a joy to see the expression on each child's face as we gave him or her gifts on behalf of their parents. It was at one of the programs that my son

Antonio turned to his mother and said, "Now I know my daddy didn't buy that fire truck for me for Christmas." All of the time he had thought that I had bought him the fire truck for Christmas.

Quite often, several faith-based and corporate sponsors beyond our church family would contribute gifts for the program. These sponsors would purchase the gifts, wrap them, and Antoinette and I would pick them up and package them in plastic bags to deliver to the families. Each year, the number of children sponsored would grow. At one point, we sponsored 1,500 children and had to reduce the number to a thousand because we lacked sufficient sponsors. *"Children are a heritage from the LORD, offspring a reward from him" (Psalm 127:3) NIV.*

We thank God that, over the years, we had five generous sponsors who have consistently contributed to the program: Lawndale Christian Community Church, Christ Church of Oak Brook, The Stein Foundation, Roscoe, and the RML Medical Center. Were it not for their generosity, Angel Tree would not have been successful. As this book goes to press, we have been offering the Angel Tree Program for more than 25 years.

Celestial Ministries Is Conceived

With the continued success of Angel Tree, Antoinette and I came to the realization that it wasn't enough to engage with these children just once a year, so she came up with the idea of broadening their horizons by teaching them music and exposing them to the outdoors. After all, many of them had not been outside the neighborhood of North Lawndale. So I started teaching them music theory and piano and Antoinette and I would take some of them camping during the summer. In time, we decided to apply for a 501c3 not-for-profit designation, and Celestial Ministries was established. *"Do not despise these small beginnings, for the LORD rejoices to see the work begin, to see the plumb line in Zerubbabel's hand" (Zechariah 4:10) NLT.*

Sheldon Clay, a gifted drummer, who was in recovery at Hope House for abusing drugs, desired to teach children to play the drums. I recruited Shawn Casselberry, who had only recently moved into the community, attended Lawndale Christian Community Church, and was also a drummer. Shawn invited his wife Jennifer, and both became members of the Celestial Ministries board.

Four months later, we applied for a grant, and soon after, one day a semi-trailer pulled up to the church with 30 to 40 drums from Yamaha. Coach Gordon asked if I was expecting a delivery, to which I replied, "Yes." I had no idea that it would arrive that day. The students were in shock, in disbelief that the drums were for them.

For several months, the students would play with their sticks on the seatbacks of chairs, but now they actually had real drums! Thus, the Celestial Ministries Drumline was formed. Girls and boys from the church signed up to join. We practiced on Saturdays because the Kingdom Women's Bible study was held concurrently, allowing the parents to bring their children with them so they wouldn't be left home alone. At the time, we didn't know what we were doing, but God did: *"What no eyes has seen, what no ears has heard, and what no human mind has conceived"— the things God has prepared for those who love him"(1 Corinthians 2:9) NIV.*

In time, the drumline got better and better, and we were invited to perform at block club parties and special events. Every week, we were performing somewhere. The highlight of our exposure as a unit was our participation in the famous Bud Billiken Parade every year, one of the largest such events in the country.

Organizing Our Board

Because we didn't have a full board, I began asking my friends if they would serve on our board. I started with Floyd Towner, who agreed without hesitation. Mrs. Mary Cray, the former teacher whom I hadn't seen in more than 30 years and ran into at a Petco, said yes, too. I asked three other friends: Pam McCain, Doris

Sims, and Donnie Graham if they would join our board, and of all agreed. Since then, God has brought some incredible people to the Celestial Ministries board. Once again, it was all by faith.

A Permanent Home for Celestial Ministries

For several years we'd operated Celestial Ministries out of The Lawndale Christian Community Church. Later, after our operation outgrew the space, we moved and began operating out of the Common House located at 18th and Springfield, directly across the way from our home. After occupying the Common House for a while, we moved into the basement of the Field House of Douglass Park. We were allowed to stay there for five months until, once again, we were forced to leave. Our next home was Blessed Sacrament Youth Center at Cermak and Central Park, which housed us for a year. It was there that God told me to look for a space of our own and gave me the vision of exactly what the place should look like.

Antoinette, Valerie Leonard, a friend and a highly respected community activist in the North Lawndale Community and co-founder of the North Lawndale Community Coordinating Council (NLCCC), and I scheduled a meeting with Coach Gordon to discuss the vacant building located directly across the street from Hope House, asking him if he could help us get it. He declined, saying that he couldn't help us. At the time, I didn't know that they had plans to buy the building themselves, to tear it down, and build a fitness center.

It didn't deter me from looking. I spotted a storefront on Cermak Road, convinced that it was the next home for Celestial Ministries, but once we took a look inside, we agreed that it was too small. As we walked out of the building, I saw that another property around the corner on 21st and Drake, located next to a school playlot was available. Surely, this must be the building, I thought!

I made several phone calls to a realtor, who called me back, saying that the building was on the market for $150,000. I didn't know how or where we were going to get the money, but I knew that with God, all things are possible.

We began praying and circling the building as we prayed. We were prepared to put $1,000 down on the building, but another buyer had outbid us. After a year, the realtor called me and said that if I still wanted the building, I could have it for $100,000. We were so happy that we hurried to put $5,000 down. Board members Shawn and Jennifer Casselberry lent us the funds for the earnest money on the condition that we pay them back later. After putting the money down, we learned that the building was in demolition court. We felt deceived by the seller because we hadn't been told. Our attorney, Sally Wagonmaker, was instrumental in helping us close the sale. We told the bank that $15,000 was all we had, and they sold it to us for $20,000. Despite our happiness in getting the building, we lacked the money to rehab it, so it remained vacant for another year.

An Angel Donor

In five years of the building being vacant, we finally got the money to begin rehabbing it when my childhood friend and member of Superior Movement Tyrone Powell had been awarded money from a lawsuit and donated a portion of it to contribute to the cause. He asked how much I needed, to which I replied, "$80,000."

At the time, I was still in seminary, and I shared with my classmates my plans to purchase a building for my ministry and told them about the generous offer, seeking their advice. They left the decision up to me, inquiring whether the money was to be a loan or a gift. I told them that it was a gift because I didn't know how I would be able pay him back if it had been a loan. I made it clear earlier that if I were given the money, I would have no way of paying it back, since the music school was a nonprofit

501c3 organization whose mission was to serve the children of North Lawndale. They bought into the vision and agreed that it was so important to the neighborhood that I should accept Tyrone's offer.

The Property Is Vandalized

After work had resumed on the building, we had a break-in. One day as I turned the corner onto Drake, I noticed that the back door to the basement was off the hinges. When I entered the building, I was afraid because I feared that the intruders might still be inside, so I made a lot of noise to frighten them away.

As I proceeded to check out the building, making as much commotion as I could to scare the burglars away, I noticed two crowbars lying on the floor. I went upstairs and discovered a sledgehammer there lying on the floor. Whoever had broken in had left, and amazingly, no damage was done to the walls or pipes. My suspicion was that whoever had broken in did so to steal the copper to sell but were unsuccessful. It looked as if they had come to destroy the place, but it was clear to me that an angel of the Lord had scared them away because it appeared as if they had dropped their tools and left.

Contractor Problems

The contractors that we had hired to complete the work were taking too long, so we called a meeting with the architect and them. When the architect arrived, he was so angry that he cursed them out for failing to follow his plans. Specifically, the stairwells were supposed to be exposed, and they had enclosed them, but it was too late to make a change, and our money was running out. As a result, we ended up firing the contractors and hired another crew.

The next general contractor we hired was the uncle of a friend. He provided us with a resume, but we never checked his references because we were new at this kind of work. The only

One we had on our side was God. The new contractor had shot us through the grease as well.

He would have me pick up three or four Mexicans at Home Depot to sand the drywall. One day, when the contractor and I had been gone for a while, upon returning he shouted for them to come down, asking what the hell they had been doing.

"We've been gone for three hours, and all you've done was this?" he yelled.

The only one who seemed to understand him was the crew leader, and even he spoke very little English. The contractor had hired sub-contractors whom he paid very little and kept a greater amount for himself. We soon found out from one of the subcontractors that he'd been lying to us about how much he was paying them. Once again, we had to fire a contractor.

Hope House Comes to the Rescue

One day during construction, dry wall was being transported by a Home Depot truck, and I stopped by Hope House to get some help unloading it. One of the men, Robert Smith, whom I didn't know at the time, told me he was a carpenter by trade. I believed him, and he said that if I paid him $60 a day, he would help me rehab the building. I accepted his offer.

As soon as he started to work I saw the amazing work that he was doing, and I could see improvement in building's rehab efforts. Every day, I would pick Robert up about 6:30 a.m., and he would work until 3:30 p.m. He installed the walls, floors, and doors. He was very talented. His son Rashaud became one of the leading drummers on our drumline.

When the time came for us install the electricity, Jack Melvin was referred to us. He and his partner put in all of the work lights, outlets, and power boxes. One day I spotted Jack at the top of a telephone pole and was afraid that he would get electrocuted.

Once he had installed the electrical wiring, we thought that all we had to do was pass the city inspection. Once again, we were thrown another curve ball when we found out that Jack wasn't a certified electrician. For us to pass the inspection, we had to have a certified electrician on site. Thank God that a friend of ours knew one who agreed to help us out. When the inspector came, he found only a few things wrong and informed us that in order to pass, they had to be corrected. Once they were, we passed the inspection.

Reggie Brown was a drywaller and a former Hope House resident who helped us with Angel Tree for many years. He was a man possessed when it came to installing drywall. He never complained and worked for us like it was a real job and he was getting paid. When I did compensate him every now and then, I could tell that he wasn't doing it for the money, and I could see his dedication in making sure the rehab was completed. I thank God for him and all the work that he put in. I loved it when people shared the vision I had because not all are going to see what you have envisioned. I had to believe in myself and in God, exercising my faith and knowing that He wanted me to succeed.

Friends and Family Pitch In

Ben Webster and Charles Blakes were two childhood friends who became professional carpenters, so I called upon them to help me. Motivated by scripture, I explained to them up front that I didn't have any money, and that the building was to be a Christian music school for the community of North Lawndale: *"Unless the LORD builds the house, the builders labor in vain" (Psalm 127:1) NIV.*

I also explained how we had seen how drugs and gangs had torn our neighborhood apart and that it would be a way of instilling hope. The two had other priorities but offered to help me when they could. One of the biggest jobs was to install an iron stairway in the hall, and they were instrumental in making it happen. I thank God for these two friends of two carpenters who freely contributed their time and skill to the cause.

Another person whom I called on during the rehab effort was my cousin Kenneth Eubanks aka (Pookie), who was at the time was struggling with substance abuse. He helped paint, drywall, and sand. He also volunteered to occupy the building with me until we were able to install a security system.

We spent many nights sleeping on the cold concrete floor and would watch movies on a tiny DVD player. I enjoyed every moment of it because I had the chance to spend time with my cousin that I wouldn't ordinarily have had. The Apostle Paul couldn't have said it any better: *"I planted the seed, Apollos watered it, but God has been making it grow"(1 Corinthians 3:6) NIV.*

The Ribbon-Cutting for Celestial Ministries

"Now to Him who is able to do exceedingly abundantly above all you could ever ask or think, according to the power that works in us."
—Ephesians 3:20 NKJV

August 15, 2014 was the date of the ribbon-cutting ceremony for The Celestial Ministries School of Fine Arts. Alderman Michael Scott, Commissioner Bobbie Steele, and a representative from Congressman Danny Davis's office were among the government officials in attendance, as well as family, friends from the community, members of Lawndale Christian Community Church, and Dr. Fleagle from Northern Theological Seminary.

We awarded plaques to Valerie Leonard, Congressman Danny Davis, Commissioner Bobbie Steele, and other community leaders for their support. A few jazz musicians whom I went to high school with performed, as well as the Celestial Ministries drumline. We served enough food to feed the whole neighborhood. A friend, Donna Holt, who worked for alderman Scott, hosted the event and made sure everything ran right. She was also working for the alderman at the time. It was a glorious day! *"Commit to the LORD whatever you do, and he will establish your plans" (Proverbs 16:3) NIV.*

The first week of classes at Celestial Ministries drew eight students, but we were encouraged: *"Do not despise these small beginnings, for the LORD rejoices to see the work begin" (Zechariah 4:10) NLT.* Five were from a family that lived around the corner. We were glad to enroll them and enjoyed having them, but they were so disrespectful that I decided to temporarily close our doors. When I reopened the next day, one of the family members asked me why I had closed. I told her that I didn't like her brothers' behavior. She replied that she had told her mother about them and had been crying because we weren't open. I realized then that some of the children had no place to go outside of their homes.

Although two other organizations that sponsor youth programs operate in the neighborhood, they aren't like Celestial Ministries, which teaches music, the Bible, and practices the love of God. We found that this is exactly what many communities need: a place where children can feel safe, be exposed to music, develop social skills, and learn about God.

Many of the children were hesitant to come to us because they thought Celestial Ministries was a church, but one by one they overcame their hesitancy because of word-of-mouth testimonies from other children.

In 2020, our sixth year, I was able see God expanding our vision. We have great students and an equally great board. We are collaborating with other ministries and organizations in the Lawndale community. The only thing we lack is a grant writer to help us secure funding for our efforts. We've been trusting God, and He has been supplying us with the resources that we need to remain open. The moment we stop trusting Him, I know it will be over because there's no way in the world we could have done all the things we've done without our trust and faith in Jesus Christ. We know this, and we stand firm on this truth. Every day in my prayers I tell God that this is His ministry and that I want Him to use it for His glory: *"The Lord is my strength and my shield; my heart trusts in him, and he helps me. My heart leaps for joy, and with my song I praise him" (Psalm 28:7) NIV.*

Water, Water Everywhere

In December 2017 while Antoinette and I were out shopping, she was prompted to stop by the Celestial Ministries building for some reason. When I raised the shutter covering the front entrance, water was rushing out the front door. When we opened the door, water was everywhere, and I didn't know where it was coming from. Following the source, I was led to the ladies' restroom where a pipe had burst. Going downstairs to the basement, I saw water pouring in. It was truly chaotic! All I could do was recite the scripture: *"No weapon forged against you shall prevail"(Isaiah 54:17) NIV.*

The blessing for us was that even with the water pouring from the ceiling, none of the furniture and computers that we had in the basement were damaged. I praised God because He continued to look after Celestial Ministries. George Clopton, a former Hope House resident, and a friend came over right away to repair the broken pipes. It was amazing to me to see how God puts people in our lives who are equipped to do the things that we can't do ourselves. It was another miracle that proved to me the faithfulness of God.

Whenever it rained, we would get water in the basement, and I tried everything I knew to correct the problem—even praying it out! I turned to God asking when He would help us to get the problem fixed, keeping in mind the scripture from Philippians 4:6-7 NKJV: *"Be anxious for nothing, but in everything by prayer and supplication, with thanksgiving, let your requests be known to God."* It was an anxious time, but I let God hear my request. His response was "Trust me."

You see, God's timing is not our timing. *"A thousand years in your sight are like a day that has just gone by, or like a watch in the night" (Psalm 90:4) NIV.*

Often, we want things to happen the way we want them to happen, but perhaps God has an agenda too, and perhaps He wants to do something so that we would know that only He could have done it.

Sometimes I found myself crying as I drained the water from the basement. After I had gotten all the water out, I had to dry the carpet. Fortunately, Hope House had two floor dryers that I borrowed to help.

Another Miracle Occurs

We had been in our location three years before an Hispanic neighbor moved in, claiming that the rearmost portion of land behind our building belonged to him. After arguing about it, we had our lawyer to look into it. One day, while I was at work, Antoinette called to tell me that some work was being done on the land behind our building. She reported that the neighbor had even involved the police, insisting that the land belonged to him.

Based on our attorney's investigation of the matter, according to the plat of survey, it appeared that the land was indeed his. We acquiesced but pointed out that his fence had been erected on land that belonged to Celestial Ministries. He then agreed to remove the fence and cemented the strip of land behind our building as well as the land behind his. After he had done so, we noticed that the flooding problem had been solved. The basement no longer floods. Once again, our faith in God manifested itself by a solution to a continuing problem.

A Garden Grows Next Door

In 2017, we acquired the land next door to our building, and Antoinette decided to plant a garden there. She had a vision for growing fruits and vegetables and distributing the harvest to the residents in the community. At the same time, she decided to teach students in the community to grow their own food. A youth group from Old St. Patrick's Catholic Church volunteered to help us plan the garden. Denise Burns was a chaperone of this group.

After several conversations with her, Antoinette persuaded her to join the board of Celestial Ministries. She accepted the invitation, and once she came aboard, she was ready to help out wherever she could. First, it was helping with Angel Tree, next it was the garden, and then she helped us spearhead a service project with our students and the youth from Old St. Patrick's, of which her daughter Allie and son John were a part.

The first project was to clean up a school from the south side of Chicago when the students were on summer break. It was an amazing thing to see black youth and white youth working together and getting to know each other. John, Denise's husband, had as much energy as he had ideas and was always ready to help out when needed. Owners of a restaurant in Indiana, they welcomed us to visit anytime we could. Antoinette and Denise developed a wonderful relationship, and I'm glad that God has placed her and John in our lives.

Celestial Ministries' Drumline Gains Popularity

Celestial Ministries' drumline was beginning to perform at large venues, making it a challenge for us to transport the students and their instruments. This forced me to call on friends to see if they could help. Often, they would help to drive the students to the performances, but once the performance was over, they weren't around to pick them up. Other times, a couple of students and I would take the drums back to Celestial Ministries first, and then I would return and pick up the rest of the students. This went on for years until a wonderful donor blessed us with a fifteen-passenger van.

Having the van made it easy to get to and from our performances without depending on someone else to pick us up. It also helped us resume our prison ministry in which Antoinette played a key role in transporting single-parent mothers to visit their loved ones in prison. She had developed a system in which she ensured that everyone going was actually on the prison's guest list. Then, she would make baskets with sandwiches, fruits, and gifts to give to them during the trip. Once they arrived, she would drop them off at the prison, returning to pick them up when it was time for them to leave.

Leading Prayer Marches in North Lawndale

With the rise of black-on-black shootings in Chicago, God placed on my heart the need to reach out to several churches in the Lawndale community to organize prayer marches as a unified response to the violence. At the time, no one had ever organized a prayer march before. A year earlier, my first-born son from a previous relationship, Stanley Jr., was shot and killed in Detroit, leaving behind four children. Not long afterwards, several sons of friends were shot and killed as a result of increasing gun violence as well.

Ashley Pharis, a young volunteer from Mission Year, a nationally known ministry that encourages and supports the involvement of youth leaders in social justice initiatives in cities helped organize the marches.

As part of the initiative, ten churches came together for the march, and each would host a march every other week. I made sure that the men from Hope House attended as well as the Celestial Ministries drumline. The drumline marched in front so that people would hear the drums and know we were coming. Behind the drummers were the men of Hope House, the alderman of the ward, and several community leaders. Following the residents of Hope House would be 75 to 100 community residents and other supporters marching.

At different corners, we paused to pray and someone who'd had a family member killed by gun violence would speak about its impact on him or her, their families, and the community. The Chicago Alternative Policing Strategy (CAPS), an arm of the Chicago Police Department created to build relationships between the community and the police department, stationed a squad car in the front and at the rear of the marchers. After the march, the host church would supply hot dogs and water, and we would fellowship with entertainment.

During the time we marched, we couldn't see its effect, but we knew that God was working behind the scenes. Perhaps someone in a gang heard us and changed his mind about shooting someone. Maybe someone who marched with us had a relative in a gang and decided to talk with him about engaging in violent behavior. Perhaps someone saw that the people in the community were coming together and didn't approve of their behavior and decided to change, or maybe someone felt guilty about a shooting that he was involved in. I don't know, but God knows, and I was just being obedient to what He had placed on my heart to do.

Ashley later got engaged and was planning her wedding when she asked if I could bring the Hope House Choir to sing at their wedding reception. Of course, there was no way I could turn her down since she had done so much for me and the Hope House ministry.

On the day of her wedding, we loaded up the bus and took a two-hour drive to Indiana. As we were bringing the instruments up the stairs, we were stopped at the front door and told that we couldn't bring the drums in. I had no idea that Ashley's or her husband-to-be's family were Amish; everyone there looked like they were. It didn't matter to us because we were there for Ashley.

When they told us that we couldn't bring the drums in, I had them get Ashley. When they finally did, she told them that it was OK to let us bring in the drums. Once we began to sing, everyone started clapping and was smiling broadly. When we left, we ended up with a flat tire on the highway and were stuck for several hours before someone came to our rescue.

I realized that when you are trying to do the will of God, there will always be those who will try everything they can to distract you from your purpose. Thus, a staff member came to me and told me that we needed to stop marching and praying and to do more to help around the church. While I agreed that the church was our first priority, I knew that God wanted us to do more. *"From everyone who has been given much, much will be demanded; and from the one who has been entrusted with much, much more will be asked" (Luke 12:48) NIV.*

I did make sure that everything was taken care of at the church before we would embark on our marches and have always put the church first, but I still had to do what I thought God wanted me to do.

Founding the Celestial Sounds Recording Studio

In 2015, our for-profit recording studio, Celestial Sounds, was formed to be a revenue stream for Celestial Ministries. My son Antwane has a business degree from SAE Institute and is the CEO. He is assisted by two interns, Alonzo Washington and Juan Diaz, young men who have been a blessing to the studio. Rappers have come from all over the city to record at Celestial Sounds, where Juan airs a podcast once a month. We keep our costs low to keep them affordable for our mainly student clientele. Our goal is to be a place where they can come and record their ideas.

A Surprise Cancer Diagnosis

In February 2018, I was dropped by my insurance coverage that I had had for nearly twelve years. Because I am a diabetic, I need insulin to help control my blood sugar level. I explained what had happened to my doctor, who led me to a social worker at Rush University Hospital, who, in turn led me to the Community Health Center, a clinic that helps people who don't have insurance for a period of three months.

I appreciated it so much because, for the three months that I had coverage, they had taken good care of me, supplying my insulin and teaching me how to better control my diabetes. After the three months, I was given an additional three months of supplies and insulin and was provided resources for where I could get health insurance.

A month later, the clinic sent me a container and asked for a stool sample. Within a month I was informed that they had found blood in my stool. In denial, I thought it was hemorrhoids, which I've had in the past.

In 2012, I had a colonoscopy, the results of which came out negative. In December 2018, I received a letter asking me to report to the Cook County Hospital for a colonoscopy. When the procedure was performed, I was informed that a tumor as well as some polyps had been detected. A biopsy was taken, and it came back negative, but the tumor had to be removed.

I had surgery in February 2019, and eleven inches of my colon was removed in addition to the tumor. Another biopsy was taken to ensure that no cancer remained. After the operation, I was hospitalized for three days with an IV and only fluids to drink.

While at the hospital, the first person to visit me was Coach Gordon whom the Holy Spirit had preordained. We had a great conversation after which he prayed for me before leaving.

Later, when I got the surgical report, I was told that the tumor was cancerous and that it was hiding under the one that had earlier been removed. It was stage one, and they said that all of it had been had removed. I praised God because, had He not intervened, I might have been walking around with cancer and the possibility of it spreading. If I had not lost my insurance and gone to the Westside Health Center for those six months, there's no telling what the outcome would have been. I thanked God for His healing power! *"Lord my God, I called to you for help, and you healed me." (Psalm 30:2) NIV.*

A Call to Serve

"He has shown you, O mortal, what is good. And what does the Lord require of you? To act justly and to love mercy and to walk humbly with your God." —Micah 6:8 NIV

Since the opening of the Celestial Ministries School of Fine Arts building in 2014, I've limited my volunteerism to other ministries so that I could concentrate on getting Celestial Ministries off the ground and make it a success. When a restorative justice court, (RJCC), the first court of its kind in the State of Illinois, was established in the North Lawndale community, I knew that I had to be a part of it.

The court is designed to help youth between the ages of 18 and 26 who are charged with a first-time nonviolent felony, and who accept responsibility for the harm they have caused. After completing the program, the ex-offender graduates, and community leaders, city, and state officials, and even the chief judge, attend the ceremony. The offender's record is expunged, his or her case is dropped, and the slate is wiped clean.

Antoinette and I both volunteered to participate and help with the court. Speaking from the point of view of an ex-offender, what a wonderful and essential program this is! As of this writing, the program is now implemented in the Austin and Englewood communities.

The first day that we attended, a former drumline student whom I hadn't seen in years, was a defendant entering the court system. Afterwards, we spoke to him, the public defender, and the social worker assigned to his case. I asked if I could be a mentor to him in helping to arrange the community service component of his restitution for wrongdoing, which is part of the restorative justice requirement. The court agreed, and afterwards, I became more and more involved.

"Peace Circles" and Restorative Justice

Every Thursday prior to a court hearing, we would attend what is called a "peace circle," located in an adjoining room to the court. The circle is open to anyone who cares to sit in it, so we might have court participants, community residents, and guests from across the city, in addition to the leader of the peace circle.

The circle gives the participants a safe place where he or she can freely express themselves and realize that they are not in this by themselves. In such an intimate setting, participants would share how they were feeling, what led them to be a part of the court, what was the worst incident they had ever experienced, what things motivated them, what was their favorite movie, and so on. We'd never know what questions would be asked. Its purpose was to make the participants relaxed and feel welcome.

In the center of the circle several objects called "talking pieces" are placed, and the rule is that no one is allowed to talk unless he or she holds the talking piece. When the person with the talking piece asks a question, he passes it to the next person who can either choose to answer the question, or pass the talking piece to the next person. No one is forced to answer any question. At times there are pretty interesting questions posed in these circles. Sometimes there is laughter, sometimes anger, and sometimes weeping. Everything that is expressed must remain within the circle and is not to be shared outside of it. All is confidential for the participants' sakes.

Today, peace circles are held throughout the week at various locations throughout the Chicagoland community. These circles are private, and only the participants can decide who may be a part of them. It is the "circle keeper's" role to ask the participants who they want to be included in their circles, the purpose of which is to help the offender attain the several goals required to complete the program. Goals may be to obtain a driver's license, complete several hours of community service at one of the Hub's organizations (a group of community organizations that has agreed to provide resources for the court's clients), obtain a GED certificate, build a stronger relationship with a family member, or obtain a job. In completing these requirements, the offender meets with a case manager, social worker, and sometimes a mentor.

"The Repair Harm" Agreement

Offenders who participate in the program must also complete a goal-setting sheet, called a "repair harm agreement," which is discussed at the circles with everyone signing it. Sometimes the person whom the defendant offended may be part of the circle, but if the person offended is absent, a resident of the community stands in his or her place as a surrogate. I have been involved in the program as a surrogate, mentor, community leader, and vehicle for a defendant's performing community service through Celestial Ministries when appropriate.

One young man whom I'll call "J.R.," was one of the first offenders introduced to me when I got involved with the program. He was very loud, used profanity, and felt that the court was a waste of his time. He expressed this to the judge, complaining that attending the court was taking him away from his job. Despite J.R.'s rudeness, the judge was lenient and compassionate towards him. Some participants approached J.R. and chided him, telling him that his behavior was out of line and that the judge could have held him in contempt.

Every time J.R. appeared in court and participated in the peace circle, we all knew that there would be trouble. After participating in the program for nine months and completing it, he became a different person.

Sitting in circles and sharing my testimony with the participants is a moving experience for me. I tell them that they don't want their cases heard at the Cook County Court Building, that it's better to have their cases heard in a restorative justice court where the people really care about them and want to see them succeed. I also tell them that I didn't go to prison for myself, but went for them, and that I have been through the system and have experienced firsthand injustices that it perpetrates on black men.

As part of the restorative justice initiative, I mentored a number of the men assigned to the court, and Antoinette has mentored several of the women. For example, a young woman whom I'll call "Lady J.", had lost custody of her children because of drugs and assault charges. Angry at her boyfriend who was at a barbershop where, coincidentally my son was having his hair cut, she broke out the windows, was arrested, and had her children taken from her. Antoinette advised her that if she wanted her children back, she would have to assume her responsibilities as a mother. It turned out that "Lady J." didn't have a stable home environment and that one of her goals was to get a job and an apartment. Antoinette assisted her in the effort, and after a year, she had successfully completed the restorative justice program and her children were returned to her.

God has given us direction on how to implement restorative justice early in the Bible when the Lord said to Moses: *"Say to the Israelites: 'Any man or woman who wrongs another in any way and so is unfaithful to the Lord is guilty and must confess the sin they have committed. They must make full restitution for the wrong they have done, add a fifth of the value to it and give it all to the person they have wronged"* (Numbers 5:6-7) NIV.

A Need for Additional Income

Even though Celestial Ministries and its music program was going well, I still struggled to pay the bills, which necessitated my seeking a part-time job. I was reminded of what Pastor Bill Winston would always say: "God strategically places us in dark places."

I learned from an online ad that that St. Malachy Catholic Church, located fifteen minutes from my home in the East Garfield Park neighborhood, was seeking a choir director and pianist. Without hesitation, I applied for the position, and within the same week was called in for an interview. I was a bit nervous, but I was reminded that God was ordering my steps. *"The LORD makes firm the steps of the one who delights in him" (Psalm 37:23) NIV.*

I knew that the Holy Spirit was leading me there, but I didn't know how it was going to turn out. I was confident that I had what it took to direct the choir because I had so much experience; however, I had never been exposed to the Catholic faith before, never having attended a mass or Catholic rite, but I was ready to learn.

I did know that I love Jesus, and if my prospective employer was OK with my background, I was ready to give them my all. The job required that I learn the traditional music Catholics sing as part of the Mass, which was fairly easy, but what made it even easier was that they wanted me to play gospel songs as well.

Their former director Mrs. Earlene Strauder, had led the choir for years, and she helped me to learn the order of service and the songs that were typically sung. I came to find out that people of the Catholic faith are some amazing people. I also have come to enjoy teaching the choir and learning about the Catholic faith. By trusting God, everything began to flow.

A Past Indiscretion Returns to Haunt Me

After a year directing the church choir, I learned that the school was looking for a music teacher to teach from pre-K to eighth grade and I applied for the position. When I was called in for the interview, I was told that since they knew me, I would be hired. I then wrestled with whether I should tell them about my previous felony or not. I couldn't lie to them, so I came right out and told them. I explained in detail how I was set up and sentenced to prison and how I was granted clemency by Governor Edgar. I was assured that I would still get the job but that they had to notify the Archdiocese of Chicago, who would look into what I had told them.

It took weeks and weeks, but the principal, Mrs. Bridget Miller, told me to be patient and to let her handle it, promising me that if they didn't approve of me by the next week, she would talk to them herself. She asked me if a gun was involved in my case, and I said yes, but that it wasn't my gun, so the charges were thrown out in court. She also asked if the incident involved children, to which I replied, no.

Somehow, the sheriff department's paperwork indicated that a gun and children were involved in the incident, which was untrue. I was required to submit a deposition attesting to that fact. I complied, submitting the documentation from the state police department that corroborated my attestation. Finally, after another week, I was called and told that I had the job. I praised God for His faithfulness. *"So do not be ashamed of the testimony about our Lord or of me his prisoner. Rather, join with me in suffering for the gospel, by the power of God" (2 Timothy 1:8) NIV.*

While working at St. Malachy, I realized that God had seen my potential and had been preparing me all along. I was now teaching music from preschool to eighth grade and was responsible for spearheading the school's Christmas and Black History programs. Throughout my surgery in 2018, the St.

Malachy administrators told me to take as much time as I needed to recover, and I really appreciated their support.

In 2019, the St. Malachy choir was invited to participate in a gospel choir competition, and while I didn't know what to expect, I knew that we had an outstanding choir. The competition was held on the south side of Chicago. After the competition, we had won first place in two categories! I couldn't wait to start the choir for the next year because I knew that it would excel. While we were planning our very first gospel concert, the Coronavirus, which resulted in a devastating pandemic that has claimed the life of a couple of friends, threw a wrench in our plans for 2020.

COVID-19 Interrupts In-Class Teaching

Because of the outbreak in early 2020, I had to learn how to teach online quickly. Schools in Chicago were closed by April, and we were forced to do the best that we could teaching the students virtually. My technology skills are limited, so my son Antwane had to help me set up Zoom meetings with my students at St. Malachy and at Celestial Ministries. It took some time, but I mastered it. Many of my students didn't have a computer or laptop at home, so I was able to work with only a few students, but they adapted to the situation well.

With Celestial Ministries closed, I provided online classes and delivered food to those in need in North Lawndale. I also took a small group of students swimming at a friend's house and hosted a small class reunion at our Celestial Ministries building. We were taking a risk, but we did so by practicing social distancing, washing our hands frequently, and wearing face masks as prescribed by the public health officials.

Drafted to Teach Physical Education

Because of the pandemic, I had to adjust my working life as did many whose jobs have been impacted by COVID-19. After I returned to St. Malachy from winter break, I was informed that although music classes were still being offered, the students weren't allowed to sing as a precaution against the further spread of the virus. Instead, I was drafted to teach physical education to pre-K through second grade. I was thankful to still have a job, and I accepted the position gracefully. I had never taught PE, but I knew some basic exercises that I could teach the students. Mrs. Miller asked what I planned to do with the students, and expressed her confidence that I'd figure something out.

Indeed I did. I had the students line up and I would tell each one to point to themselves and say the words, "God loves me." I would have them to repeat it, followed by the words, "I'm special. I'm real special!" I would then ask them why they were special, to which they would respond "Because God made me!" I would affirm them by telling them, "That's right. God made you. He loves you, and He has a plan for your life."

After this affirmation, I would have them memorize a verse from the Bible, have them recite it several times, and then end with an exercise routine that included jumping jacks, arm rotations, toe touches, and sit-ups. After allowing them fifteen minutes of free time, I would then have them to split up into teams for relay races, followed by games of "Simon Says," or "Duck, Duck, Goose." As a team player, I had to adjust to the new demands that the school required in the face of a world-wide health crisis that has taken an incalculable toll on students and the way they are taught.

The Impact of COVID-19 on Celestial Ministries

Adjusting to the pandemic while operating Celestial Ministries also was a challenge for me, as I had to stop in-person classes at the building. Paul Isihara, a friend, long-time supporter of Celestial Ministries, and professor at Wheaton College, suggested that he and his brother sponsor a computer programming and violin class at Celestial Ministries to be held once a week for twelve weeks. The classes would be taught via Zoom. Upon completion of the courses, the students would receive a certificate of completion and a $100.00 stipend.

A mutual friend of ours, Sarah Torrenga, and a co-worker at Paul's sister's music school in Boston, Kenneth Mok, agreed to teach the violin lessons. Paul and a former Wheaton College alumnus would teach the computer programming classes. I added a piano class to accommodate two students of Celestial Ministries who wanted to continue their piano lessons during the pandemic.

Observing that numerous families from the North Lawndale community were having difficulty feeding their children, I approached one of the sponsors of Celestial Ministries, Cliff Bregstone, founder of Consortium for Communities, to buy food for ten families each month. We took on the task of picking up the groceries from Costco, apportioning the items per family, and then delivering them. The recipients of the groceries were grateful beyond expression when receiving the food. My hope and prayer in trying to alleviate the hunger and pain that has been exacerbated by the pandemic is that they might come to know Christ better, and might encourage their children or grandchildren to consider joining the music program at Celestial Ministries.

Black Lives Matter Protests Come to North Lawndale

"For he himself is our peace, who has made the two groups one and has destroyed the barrier, the dividing wall of hostility."
—*Ephesians 2:14 NIV*

On May 25, 2020, a 46-year-old black Minnesotan, George Floyd, was asphyxiated by a Minneapolis policeman who knelt on his neck for allegedly trying to pass a counterfeit bill, sparking mass protests across the nation. The barbaric murder as the victim cried out for his mother and begged for his life was caught on video to the nation's horror. The three policemen involved in the incident were fired, and as of this writing, the lead officer has been convicted of murdering Floyd and sentenced to 22 and a half years in prison, while his accomplices are charged with second-degree murder and aiding and abetting a second-degree murder.

On May 30, in response to the modern-day lynching, rioting came to my North Lawndale neighborhood. My community hadn't recovered from the riots that broke out in the wake of Rev. Dr. Martin Luther King's assassination in 1968, 52 years before, but because of the frustration and rage at yet another killing of a black man, residents vandalized and looted businesses in North

Lawndale and across the city, setting fire to grocery stores, clothing stores, gas stations, and currency exchanges. I spent the night at the Celestial Ministries building to prevent it from being harmed. Had it been targeted, I believe my ministry teaching music to the children of the North Lawndale community would have been over. I had faith that it would be left unscathed, but knowing that I was there to protect it brought me a sense of security.

Before I went home early the next morning, the Holy Spirit prompted me to drive around to survey the damage to my neighborhood. As I did, tears fell from my eyes. I was hurting, and I couldn't ask God why because I knew why. I knew that it was because of pent-up anger, helplessness, and frustration. I also knew that some of the participants in the rioting and looting were just capitalizing on the peaceful marches that sprung up to protest George Floyd's killing. Many of the protestors lived outside of the neighborhood and used it as a chance to loot.

Rev. James Brooks, pastor of Harmony Community Church and Chief Ministry Officer at Lawndale Christian Health Center and Michael Scott, the alderman of the 24th Ward, appealed to residents of the community to help clean up the rubbish that was left in the aftermath of the outbreak. Antoinette persuaded me to help, so I did. I went to the corner of Pulaski and Roosevelt Roads, grabbed a black plastic garbage bag, and began helping collect the debris from the parking lot. A young white man joined me and began to help. We ended up collecting three bags of garbage, and afterwards, went to the next destination.

We met everyone at 19th Street and Pulaski at a gas station that had been set on fire the night before. After we cleaned up, the volunteer who had helped me, along with his friend stayed behind and struck up a conversation with me. It happened that he attended a church on the North Side, where he lived. His friend, however, lived in one of the buildings in the neighborhood. I thanked them because they didn't have to risk their safety to do what they did.

The following month, blacks and Hispanics from North and South Lawndale, held a peace march in Douglas Park (recently re-named Douglass Park in honor of the African American orator and abolitionist Frederick Douglass and his wife Julia). The Celestial Ministries drumline was invited to participate in the event, but I declined because some of my students' parents were uncomfortable with it. For my part, I felt that the rally was much needed because during the civil unrest that accompanied the killing of George Floyd, compounded by the murders of Breonna Taylor and Ahmaud Arbery, blacks in North Lawndale were burning up businesses in their own community while Hispanics were in the streets and on the sidewalks standing guard in front of their businesses in South Lawndale. Even gang members were chanting and wielding baseball bats, and I was caught in the middle of it. I started praying as I was driving, keeping my eyes in front of me and hoping that none of them noticed me driving through their neighborhood. When I got back to Pulaski Road, I took a deep breath because a police car was stationed there.

In several incidents, blacks were attacking Hispanics, and Hispanics were attacking blacks, so the idea of a peace rally would help foster closer relationships between the two communities. The day before the rally, I took the drumline to perform for an eighth-grade graduation parade at St. Malachy School, which pleased the students because they couldn't have a normal graduation because of COVID-19. After the parade, I treated them to pizza at Little Caesars.

A Dialogue on Race Relations

Because of the tension between the blacks and Hispanics, the peace rally was a step closer toward uniting us. In late summer 2020, a friend, Mike Trout, who also was a co-worker and college coordinator at the Lawndale Christian Development Cooperation, invited about fifteen white men from affluent west suburban Hinsdale to a gathering in his backyard. We engaged in a serious conversation about what they could do to help improve race relations in our country. I could tell that not everyone was on board with the meeting, because once the group had disbanded, the white men gathered into their groups to have their own discussion. There was one black guy in their group but he left before we were told to break off into groups.

The following day, I participated in a Zoom Bible study along with at least 200 other Christian men from around the Chicago area. When this large group broke up into smaller groups, I was part of a group of six whites, two of whom were part of the gathering at Mike's house and who shared how good they felt the meeting had gone. I wanted to say that I had also attended the gathering at Mike's house and wanted to express my opinion, but they didn't acknowledge my presence, over talked me, and never once recognized me for being part of the group. I expressed my feelings to Mark Myers, a good friend of mine, who suggested that I discuss how I felt with an older black friend of his. I told Mark that I needed to talk with the small group leaders who were his neighbors to let them know how I felt, since the purpose of the gathering was to address the issue of white racism.

I tried talking to one of my white friends about my experience, but he refused to see it from my perspective. I don't know if it was because he was biased or not. I thought that since he was a dear friend, he would give me some good feedback, but all I got from him was that I wasn't seeing it his way. I also talked with a group of white Christians who hold Bible study class that I participated in on Thursday mornings. They were willing to discuss the issue to try to understand the effects of systemic racism.

The Effects of Systemic Racism on My Life

Earlier in this book, I described how systemic racism has impacted my life, and in the previous paragraph showed just how some whites, well-meaning though they might be, can be in denial that it actually exists. My life, like that of many black ex-offenders, illustrates just how insidious it can be.

I hold a master's and bachelor's degree, but still was denied consideration for jobs that I was qualified for because of race and my being stigmatized as an ex-offender. As a case in point, a large congregation in west suburban Chicago where I knew several people who I thought knew me fairly well, denied me consideration for an open position in the music department more than three times. I finally gave up, having concluded that because of my race and background, there was no need for me to continue pursuing it. It had become obvious to me that they didn't want a black worship leader in spite of my belief that the Lord wanted to use me to bring blacks and whites together through music.

Another instance involved another popular multicultural church to which I applied several times for the position of worship leader. Once again, I was qualified and had years of experience, but this church like the one before it denied me the position. After these disappointments, and after talking it over with God, I told Him that if they didn't want the good music that he had blessed me with the ability to share, then it was their loss. I knew deep inside that I was capable of bringing great worship music to any institution that would hire me, yet because of racism, I was denied the chance to use my God-given talent for the Kingdom.

Racism's Effect on Not-for-Profit Organizations

Systemic racism is embedded in just about every institution in America and is manifested in the funding opportunities for organizations located in poor communities. In North Lawndale, for instance, the large not-for-profit organizations whose leadership is primarily white are far more successful at attracting grants and other forms of funding to support their programs than smaller organizations led primarily by blacks.

Debra Brown, who co-directs a basketball ministry, "The Investment," with her husband Darrin, remarked in a conversation that it was a shame that it took a funder outside of Illinois to recognize the work that she and her husband Darrin have been doing with the youth in North Lawndale for years. They got the children involved in basketball and are constantly involved in their lives, taking them on trips and encouraging them to do well in school, but it took the University of Notre Dame to recognize them for their efforts.

But even without the recognition, they maintain that they would continue to do it because of their love for and commitment to the youth of North Lawndale. It's alright though, because to God be the glory. He knows the hearts and minds of many small organizations like Celestial Ministries, and He will continue to take care of us. *"The glory of this present house will be greater than the glory of the former house," says the LORD Almighty. "And in this place, I will grant peace, declares the LORD Almighty" (Haggai 2:9) NIV.*

It is for similar reasons as the Browns' that I founded Celestial Ministries with the goal of raising musicians for the Kingdom. In an effort to promote Celestial Ministries, throughout the greater North Lawndale community, I reached out to the pastors in the community to encourage them to send some of their youth to my school. Only a few of them took me up on my offer. Although Celestial Ministries may have gotten off to a slow start, I am confident that God is going to broaden its territory, and Celestial Ministries will become what He has intended it to be.

My father, Arthur E. Ratliff

My mother, Linnie M. Ratliff

The Penn School Band; Author top row, third from left

Author at age 13; top row, third from right

Author as a freshman at Farragut High

Author and mother at 8th grade graduation

Author at age 13

Farragut High School

The Superior Movement, from left, Author, Tyrone Powell,
Calvin Ford, Billy Avery, and David Williams

The Superior Movement, from left, David Williams, Tyrone Powell,
Billy Avery, Author and Gregory Spears

Author and wife Antoinette

Antoinette Ratliff

Wayne Gordon officiates author and wife exchanging
vows

Author and wife's wedding reception

The Ujima Condominium Association,
Author's North Lawndale home

Author's first recorded CD,
"Choose Christ" featuring Author &
"The Voices of Lawndale"

Hope House, co-founded by Author

Hope House Men's Choir;
Author front and center flanked by pastoral team

Musician and friend Dr. Darryl Saffore

Hope House Men's Choir

Author with Dr. Jill Fleagle
of Northern Seminary

Friends and supporters Bill and Nan Barnhart,
and Carrie Moore

Author, left, and youth from Lawndale Community in Romania

The Testimony of an Ex-Offender

Author receiving Jefferson Award. Left to right, Dick Johnson
WMAQ-TV, Mary Cray, Donnie Graham, wife Antoinette,
and Sen. Barack Obama

Author and Sen. Barack Obama

Author with Sen. Barack Obama
receiving Jefferson Award

Author and son Andrew

From left, Author with sons Antwane, Andrew and Antonio
and brother Randy

Celestial Ministries Building

Summer Bible Study Program led by Author

Music Class at Celestial Ministries

Author with friends and supporters
Tom Kennington and Paul Newman

Author with family; from left: siblings Arthur, Al Jose, Janice,
Lynette; niece Jennifer, brother Randy and sister Mildred

Antoinette with supporters Allie and Denise Burns

Author with V103 radio personality
Joe Soto

Author and family vacationing in Mexico

Author participating in food distribution

Celestial Ministries Drumline

Drumline marching during COVID-19 pandemic

Author, top row, far right, and extended family

Author and cousin Billy Avery
of The Superior Movement

Celestial Sounds Studio

Author teaching music at Celestial Ministries

Author and student Shamarey Cobbins
at St. Malachy school graduation

Author aboard cruise ship Spirit of Chicago
on Lake Michigan

Afterword

In this book, I tried to capture the trajectory of my life from my earliest memories of my childhood to the present day. Throughout, I endeavored to show the central role that my faith has played in my life. I have sought to present a picture of a complete life with all of its imperfections and triumphs. In doing so, I tried to show through the events of my life that in spite of being born and raised in a community that has been held up by media accounts as exemplifying the many pathologies of a permanent underclass in America, that stories of success do exist in North Lawndale and that I tried to play a role, however small in contributing to them.

I want the readers of this book to know that we all will have trials and tribulations in our lives. Some sent by Satan, some by God to build character and to strengthen us, and some we create for ourselves by abusing our free will. However, there is a loving and living God who knows all about us, and He is watching and waiting to bring us through each of them. Throughout these trials God is calling us to come near to Him because he desires to be included in every aspect of our lives. We have plans, but He has plans for our lives as well. It's our decision as to whose plans we choose to follow, but if we choose His way, we will find that it's the better way in every instance.

I hope that after reading this book, you will know the importance of faith in our lives. No matter who you are or where you are from, by having faith in God and acting in concert with his will, you will always surmount any obstacles placed in your path. I said earlier in this book, that some people are placed in our lives for a season, whether it be long or short. The important thing is to be aware of how we treat them, for we will never know how God will bless the relationships that we have created. I pray that you have profited in some way by reading about my faith journey, and if so, to God be the all the glory!

About the Author

Stanley Ratliff has been a pillar in the North Lawndale community for more than 30 years. After embarking on a music career with his high school singing group "Superior Movement" and releasing the album "Key to Your Heart," which made the music charts in the 1980s and attracted notice from the R & B music industry, he found himself imprisoned for a crime he was falsely accused of. After two-and-a half years, he was granted clemency and, upon his release, he co-founded "Hope House," a Christian recovery home for inmates who were recently released from prison and struggled with substance abuse.

He received a bachelor of arts degree in music from Northeastern Illinois University while imprisoned at the Dixon Correctional Center, and in 2014 received a master of arts degree in Christian Ministry from Northern Seminary. In 2006, Stanley and his wife Antoinette established the music ministry "Celestial Ministries" to serve children of the incarcerated as well as other underprivileged children in the North Lawndale community. Currently, he uses his gifts teaching music at St. Malachy School, The Lawndale Christian Community Church, and other respected institutions in the North Lawndale Community.

Stanley has received numerous leadership awards, including The North Lawndale Spirit of Youth Development Award, The National Jefferson Award, and the Jacqueline Kennedy Onassis Award.

He is the writer and producer of two Christian CDs: "Choose Christ," his first, by Stanley Ratliff & The Voices of Lawndale and "I Will Ever Sing Your Praise" by The Hope House Men's Choir. He is the author of the book, *A Dream, A Goal, Never A Reality*, published in 2008.

Stanley continues to live in the community where he was raised, along with his wife Antoinette. He is the father of three sons Antonio, Antwane, and Andrew, all of whom are involved with the day-to-day operations of Celestial Ministries.